THE CIVIL LIABILITY ACTS

Anthony Kerr

M.A. (Dub.), LL.M. (Lond.), of King's Inns, Barrister,
Statutory Lecturer in Law, University College Dublin

ROUND HALL

Sweet & Maxwell

Published in 1999 by
Round Hall Sweet & Maxwell
Brehon House, 4 Upper Ormond Quay,
Dublin 7.

Typeset by
Gilbert Gough Typesetting, Dublin.

Printed by
Colourbooks, Dublin.

ISBN 1–899738–92–4

A catalogue record for this book
is available from the British Library.

Preface

The Civil Liability Act 1961 was designed to reform the law as to civil liability. It amended and consolidated the law relating to the survival of causes of action on death, it amended and declared the law concerning concurrent fault, it re-enacted the statutory provisions in regard to damages for the benefit of the dependants of persons fatally injured and it made certain miscellaneous amendments to the law relating to wrongdoing. The Act has been described as being a statute of unique detail and complexity and one which is very difficult and sometimes impossible to construe. Indeed the late Judge Michael Sweeney once referred to it as "a catalogue of metaphysical conundra". Similar legislation in Australia was described by Gaudron and Gummow JJ. of the High Court of Australia, in their joint judgment in *James Hardie & Coy Pty Ltd v. Seltsam Pty Ltd* (1998) 73 A.L.J.R. 238 at 240, as having become "notorious for the conceptual and practical difficulties it engenders".

In the four decades it has been in effect, the Act has not only been amended, both in 1964 and 1996, but it has also generated a considerable body of case law, some of which has remained unreported. This book contains the up-to-date text of the legislation with all amendments, adaptations and repeals clearly shown. Each section of the 1961 and 1964 Acts is fully annotated by reference to the available jurisprudence and cross-referenced. Where appropriate, consideration has been given to foreign case law, principally English and Canadian, where the relevant statutory provisions are similar. My modest hope is that the book will be found of some use by practitioners and students of law.

Grateful appreciation is due to a large number of individuals for assistance provided and encouragement offered. A considerable debt of gratitude is due to Patrick MacEntee S.C., Q.C., not least for drawing my attention to the above-cited *dictum* of Judge Sweeney. I would specifically like to thank the late Professor James Brady, Jack Fitzgerald S.C., James O'Reilly S.C., Michael M. Collins S.C., Gerard Hogan S.C., Aedemar Kirrane, Lorraine Scully, Marcus Daly and Tony Eklof. Particular words of appreciation are also due to Pearse Sreenan for his note of the *Dennehy* judgment, which is reproduced as Appendix One and to Michael MacGrath, who originated this project some years ago.

Any omissions or errors of analysis that remain are, of course, my own. Although every effort has been made to ensure that the information given in this book is accurate, no legal responsibility, however, is accepted by the author or the publishers for any errors or omissions in that information or otherwise.

The commentary to the legislation is based on materials and information available to me at January 31, 1999.

Tony Kerr
Dublin
St Benedict's Day 1999

Table of Cases

"Al Tabith", *The* [1993] 2 Lloyd's Rep. 214 57
"Albany", *The* [1983] 2 Lloyd's Rep. 185 57
A. & P. (Ireland) Ltd v. Golden Vale Products Ltd., unreported,
    High Court, December 7, 1978 29
Alford v. Magee (1952) 85 C.L.R. 437 65
Alliance & Leicester Building Society v. Edgestop Ltd [1993]
    1 W.L.R. 1462; [1994] 2 All E.R. 38 42
Ashton v. Turner [1981] Q.B. 137; [1980] 3 W.L.R. 736; [1980]
    3 All E.R. 870 67

Baker v. Bolton (1808) 1 Camp 493; 170 E.R. 1033 4
Ball v. Kraft (1966) 60 D.L.R. (2d) 35 62
Bank of Ireland v. O'Keeffe, unreported, High Court, December 3,
    1986 .... 9, 10
Bennet v. Bennet (1879) L.R. 10 Ch. 474 58
Bennett v. Tugwell [1971] 2 Q.B. 267; [1971] 2 W.L.R. 847; [1971]
    2 All E.R. 248 43
Bewley Ryan & Company v. Cruess-Callaghan, unreported,
    High Court, January 16, 1974 42
Bitumen & Oil Refineries (Australia) Ltd v. Commissioner for
    Government Transport (1955) 92 C.L.R. 200 23
Blake v. Midland Railway Co. (1852) 18 Q.B. 93; 118 E.R. 35;
    88 R.R. 543 63
Boles v. O'Connor, unreported, High Court, February 21, 1964 12
Bondarenko v. Sommers (1968) 69 S.R. (N.S.W.) 269 67
Borough of Bathurst v. Macpherson (1879) 4 App. Cas. 256 73
Bourke v. Córas Iompair Éireann [1967] I.R. 319 76
Bradburn v. Great Western Railway Co (1874) L.R. 10 Ex. 1 80
Brambles Construction Pty Ltd v. Helmers (1966) 114 C.L.R. 213 37
Browning v. War Office [1963] 1 Q.B. 750; [1963] 2 W.L.R. 52;
    [1962] 3 All E.R. 1089 80
Buckle v. Baywater Road Board (1936) 57 C.L.R. 259 73
Buckley v. Lynch [1987] I.R. 6 ....
Budget Rent-A-Car Pty Ltd v. Van Der Kemp [1984] 3
    N.S.W.L.R. 303 62
Burton v. West Suffolk County Council [1960] 1 Q.B. 72; [1960]
    2 W.L.R. 745; [1960] 2 All E.R. 26 73
Byrne v. Ireland [1972] I.R. 241 71
Byrne v. Lancaster [1958] Ir. Jur. Rep. 51 15
Byrne v. Triumph Engineering Ltd [1982] I.R. 220; [1982]
    I.L.R.M. 317 15

Capps v. Miller [1989] 1 W.L.R. 839; [1989] 2 All E.R. 333 41

Carleton v. O'Regan, unreported, High Court, October 14, 1996 57
Carroll v. Clare County Council [1975] I.R. 221 .... 24, 41
Carroll v. Fulflex International Co Ltd, unreported, High Court,
    October 18, 1995 32
Carroll v. Purcell (1961) 107 C.L.R. 73 .... 32, 62
Cayzer, Irvine & Co v. Carron Co (1884) 9 App. Cas. 873; 54 L.J.P. 18;
    52 LT 361; 5 Asp. MLC 371 40
Clancy v. North End Garage (Wexford) Ltd [1969] I.R. 122 15
Clay v. Pooler [1982] 3 All E.R. 570 61
Clements v. Tyrone County Council [1905] 2 I.R. 415 72
Coe Estate v. Tennant (1988) 31 B.C.L.R. (2d) 236; 12 A.C.W.S.
    (3d) 97 63
Colborn v. Patmore (1834) 1 C.M. & R. 73; 3 L.J. Ex. 317 67
Connolly v. Casey, unreported, High Court, June 12, 1998 .... 31, 33
Connolly v. Dundalk UDC, unreported, Supreme Court,
    November 18, 1992 24
Conole v. Redbank Oyster Co [1976] I.R. 191 23
Conway v. Irish National Teachers' Organisation [1991] 2 I.R. 305;
    [1991] I.L.R.M. 497 .... 8, 18
Cook v. Lewis [1951] S.C.R. 830; [1952] 1 D.L.R. 1 12
Cooke v. Walsh [1984] I.L.R.M. 208 82
Cooper v. Egan, unreported, High Court, December 20, 1990 .... 62, 63
Cooper v. Miller (1994) 113 D.L.R. (4th) 1 81
Coppinger v. Waterford County Council [1996] 2 I.L.R.M. 427 46
Cornish v. Watson [1968] W.A.R. 198 62
Cowley v. Newmarket Local Board [1892] A.C. 345; 62 L.J.Q.B. 65;
    67 L.T. 486 72
Cullen v. Clein [1970] I.R. 146 29
Cunningham v. Wheeler (1994) 113 D.L.R. (4th) 1 81
Cutler v. McPhail [1962] 2 Q.B. 292; [1962] 2 W.L.R. 1135;
    [1962] 2 All E.R. 474 20

D'Arcy v. Roscommon County Council, unreported, Supreme Court,
    January 11, 1991 33
Daly v. Avonmore Creameries Ltd [1984] I.R. 131 55
Davies v. Mann (1842) 10 M. & W. 546; 12 L.J. Ex. 10; 62 R.R. 698;
    152 E.R. 588 65
Dawson v. M'Clelland [1899] 2 I.R. 486 17
Dellabarca v. Northern Storemen and Packers Union [1989]
    2 N.Z.L.R. 734 42
Dennehy v. Nordic Cold Storage Ltd, unreported, High Court,
    May 8, 1991 .... 81, Appendix One
Dillon v. MacGabhann, unreported, High Court, July 24, 1995 .... 30, 31
Doherty v. Bowaters Irish Wallboard Mills Ltd [1968] I.R. 277 81
Donnelly v. Joyce [1974] Q.B. 454; [1973] 3 W.L.R. 514; [1974]
    3 All E.R. 475 81
Donohue v. Brown [1986] I.R. 90 47
Doody v. Federation Insurance Ltd (1977) 16 S.A.S.R. 173 62

Dowling v. Armour Pharmaceutical Co Inc [1996] 2 I.L.R.M. 417 31
Dowling v. Jedos Ltd., unreported, Supreme Court, March 30, 1977.... 62, 63
Dube v. Labar (1986) 27 D.L.R. (4th) 653 44
Duck v. Mayeu [1892] 2 Q.B. 511 20
Duffy v. Fahy [1960] Ir. Jur. Rep. 69 42
Duffy v. Newsgroup Newspapers Ltd [1992] 2 I.R. 369; [1992]
    I.L.R.M. 835 15
Dunne v. Honeywell Control Systems Ltd [1991] I.L.R.M. 595 55
Dunne v. PJ White Construction Co Ltd [1989] I.L.R.M. 803 74

Eastman v. South West Thames Regional Health Authority [1991]
    R.T.R. 389 41
Egger v. Viscount Chelmsford [1965] 1 Q.B. 248; [1964] 3 W.L.R. 714;
    [1964] 3 All E.R. 406 13
Eglantine Inn Ltd v. Smith [1948] N.I. 48 13
Ennis v. McKenna Distributors Ltd, unreported, High Court,
    November 19, 1965 76

Fabre v. Arenales (1992) 27 N.S.W.L.R. 437 69
Feeney v. Ging, unreported, High Court, December 17, 1982 65
Felloni v. Dublin Corporation [1998] 1 I.L.R.M. 133 42
Fisher v. Smithson (1978) 17 S.A.S.R. 223 61
Fitzpatrick v. Furey, Irish Times Law Report, August 31, 1998
    (High Court, June 12, 1998) 61
Fitzsimons v. Bord Telecom Éireann [1991] 1 I.R. 536;
    [1991] I.L.R.M. 276 .... 62, 63
Fleming v. Kerry County Council [1955–56] Ir. Jur. Rep. 71 42
Fletcher v. National Mutual Life Nominees Ltd [1990] 1 N.Z.L.R. 97 42
Fookes v. Slayter [1978] 1 W.L.R. 1293; [1979] 1 All E.R. 137 43
Forsyth v. Evans [1980] N.I. 230 73
Froom v. Butcher [1976] Q.B. 286; [1975] 3 W.L.R. 379; [1975]
    3 All E.R. 520 41

Gala v. Preston (1991) 172 C.L.R. 243; 65 A.L.J.R. 366 .... 68, 69
Gallagher v. Electricity Supply Board [1933] I.R. 558 .... 61, 62, 63
Gammell v. Wilson [1982] A.C. 27; [1981] 2 W.L.R. 248; [1981]
    1 All E.R. 578 8
Gay O'Driscoll Ltd v. Kotsonouris, unreported, High Court,
    December 15, 1986 50
"Gaz Fountain", The [1987] 2 Lloyd's Rep. 151 57
George v. Dowling (1992) 59 S.A.S.R. 291 68
George Wimpey & Co Ltd v. British Overseas Airways Corporation
    [1955] A.C. 169; [1954] 3 W.L.R. 932; [1954] 3 All E.R. 661 23
Gillespie v. Fitzpatrick [1970] I.R. 102 .... 26, 52
Gillespie v. Fitzpatrick (No. 2), unreported, High Court, April 27, 1970 3
Gilmore v. Windle, unreported, High Court, April 10, 1965;
    [1967] I.R. 323 (S.C.) 4, 29, 30
Golden Vale plc v. Food Industries plc [1996] 2 I.R. 221 32

Goodburn v. Thomas Cotton Ltd [1968] 1 Q.B. 845; [1968]
  2 W.L.R. 229; [1968] 1 All E.R. 518 62
Graham v. Baker (1961) 106 C.L.R. 340 80
Green v. Russell [1959] 2 Q.B. 226; [1959] 3 W.L.R. 17; [1959]
  2 All E.R. 525 65
Greene v. Hughes Haulage Ltd [1997] 3 I.R. 109 .... 65, 79
Griffiths v. Kerkemeyer (1977) 139 C.L.R. 161 .... 81, 82
Grogan v. Ferrum Trading Co. Ltd [1996] 2 I.L.R.M. 216 32
Guy v. Policy Authority for Northern Ireland, unreported, N.I.Q.B.D.,
  April 14, 1989 81
Guy v. Trizec Equities Ltd (1979) 99 D.L.R. (3d) 243 80

Hall v. Herbert (1993) 101 D.L.R. (4th) 129 69
Hallahan v. Keane and Harrington [1992] I.L.R.M. 595 33
Hamill v. Oliver [1977] I.R. 73 41
Harbinson v. Armagh County Council [1902] 2 I.R. 538 72
Hardy v. Caffrey, The Irish Times, February 11, 1987 67
Hawkins v. Ian Ross (Cashings) Ltd [1970] 1 All E.R. 180 42
Hay v. Hughes [1975] Q.B. 790; [1974] 2 W.L.R. 34; [1975]
  1 All E.R. 257 63
Hayden v. Hayden [1992] 1 W.L.R. 9896; [1992] 4 All E.R. 681 63
Hayes v. Brisbane City Council (1980) 5 Q.L. 269 73
Heydon's Case (1612) 11 Co. Rep. 5a 17
Hillen v. ICL (Alkali) Ltd [1934] 1 K.B. 455 67
Hoebergen v. Koppens [1974] 2 N.Z.L.R. 597 42
Hollywood v. Cork Harbour Commissioners [1992] 1 I.R. 457 58
Holman v. Johnston (1755) 1 Cowp 341; 98 E.R. 1120 67
Holmes v. Dursley Ltd [1997] *Irish Law Log Weekly*, No 28/97, p. 311 49
Honan v. Syntex (Ireland) Ltd, unreported, High Court,
  October 22, 1990 82
Horgan v. Buckley [1938] I.R. 115 61
Horwell v. London Omnibus Co (1877) 2 Ex. D. 365 61
Hunt v. Severs [1993] Q.B. 815; [1993] 3 W.L.R. 558; [1993]
  4 All E.R. 180 (CA); [1994] 2 A.C. 350; [1994]
  2 W.L.R. 602 (HL) 23, 82
Hutton v. Philippi [1982] I.L.R.M. 578 9

Iarnród Éireann v. Ireland [1996] 3 I.R. 321; [1995] 2 I.L.R.M.
  161 (H.C.); [1996] 2 I.L.R.M. 500 (S.C.) 14
*International Commercial Bank plc v. Insurance Corporation of
  Ireland* [1989] I.L.R.M. 788 .... 4, 33
Italiano v. Barbaro (1993) 114 A.L.R. 21 69

Jackson v. Harrison (1978) 138 C.L.R. 438; 52 A.L.J.R. 474 67
James Hardie & Coy Pty Ltd v. Seltsam Pty Ltd (1998)
  73 A.L.J.R. 238 23
Jameson v. Central Electricity Generating Board [1999] 2 W.L.R. 141;

[1999] 1 All E.R. 193 19
Johnson v. Larkin [1926] 2 I.R. 40 17
Johnston v. Fitzpatrick [1992] I.L.R.M. 269 33
Judge v. Reap [1968] I.R. 217 43

Kars v. Kars (1996) 71 A.L.J.R. 107; 187 C.L.R. 354 82
Kelly v. Mayo County Council [1964] I.R. 315 72
Kelly v. The Governors of St. Laurence's Hospital [1989]
    I.L.R.M. 877 4
Kennedy v. East Cork Foods Ltd [1973] I.R. 244 55
*Keough v. Henderson Highway Branch No 215 of the Royal Canadian
    Legion* (1978) 91 D.L.R. (3d) 507 65
Knowles Estate v. Walton Estate (1992) 93 D.L.R. (4th) 734;
    69 B.C.L.R. (2d) 139 65

Lavender v. Diamints Ltd [1949] 1 K.B. 585 42
Lawless v. Bus Éireann [1994] 1 I.R. 474 48
Lawless v. Dublin Port and Docks Board [1998] I.L.R.M. 514 57
Lewicki v. Brown & Root Wimpey Highland Fabricators Ltd [1996]
    I.R.L.R. 565 80
Li v. Yellow Cab Company (1975) 532 P. 2d 1226 41
Liffen v. Watson [1940] K.B. 556 79
Littlewood v. George Wimpey & Co Ltd [1953] 2 Q.B. 501; [1953]
    3 W.L.R. 553; [1953] 2 All E.R. 915 37
Longden v. British Coal Corporation [1995] I.C.R. 957 (CA);
    [1998] A.C. 653; [1997] 3 W.L.R. 1335; [1998] I.C.R. 26 (HL) 80
Lynch v. Beale, unreported, High Court, November 23, 1974 12
Lynch v. Lynch, unreported, High Court, November 24, 1976 3

Macauley v. Minister for Posts and Telegraphs [1966] I.R. 345 .... 49, 71
McCarthy v. Walsh [1965] I.R. 246 .... 58, 64
McCauley v. McDermott [1997] 2 I.L.R.M. 486 49
McComiskey v. McDermott [1974] I.R. 75 43
McCord v. Electricity Supply Board [1980] I.L.R.M. 153 42
McDonagh v. McDonagh [1992] 1 I.R. 119; [1992] I.L.R.M. 841 .... 62, 63
McElwaine v. Hughes, unreported, High Court, April 30, 1997 30
McIntyre v. Lewis [1991] 1 I.R. 121 .... 8, 18
McKenna v. Best Travel Ltd, unreported, High Court,
    December 17, 1996 81
McKinley v. Minister for Defence [1992] 2 I.R. 333 46
McSorley v. O'Mahony, unreported, High Court, November 6, 1996 21
Maher v. Great Northern Railway Co (No. 2) (1942) 76 I.L.T.R. 189 15
Mahon v. Burke [1991] 2 I.R. 495; [1991] I.L.R.M. 59 .... 8, 59, 61
Malone v. Great Northern Railway Co [1931] I.R. 1; 65 I.L.T.R. 57 15
March v. E & M Stramare Pty Ltd (1991) 65 A.L.J.R. 334 65
Mead v. Clarke Chapman & Co Ltd [1956] 1 W.L.R. 76; [1956]
    1 All E.R. 44 62

Merlihan v. AC Pope Ltd [1946] 1 K.B. 106 37
Merryweather v. Nixan (1799) 8 T.R. 186 22
Morris v. Murray [1991] 2 Q.B. 6; [1991] 2 W.L.R. 195; [1990]
   3 All E.R. 801 44
Moynihan v. Greensmyth [1977] I.R. 55 10
Mullen v. Doyle, unreported, Supreme Court, May 10, 1967 32
Murphy v. Cronin [1966] I.R. 699; 102 I.L.T.R. 57 62
Murphy v. Hennessy [1984] I.R. 378; [1985] I.L.R.M. 100 50
Murphy v. J. Donohoe Ltd [1992] I.L.R.M. 378 .... 3, 19, 20
Murphy v. Times Newspapers Ltd, unreported, Supreme Court,
   October 21, 1997 15
Murray v. Minister for Finance, unreported, Supreme Court,
   April 21, 1982 71

National Insurance Co. of New Zealand Ltd v. Espagne (1961)
   105 C.L.R. 569 82
Naum v. Nominal Defendant [1974] 2 N.S.W.L.R. 14 .... 62, 63
Neville v. Margan Ltd, unreported, High Court, December 1, 1988 ...... 29, 37
Nevin v. Roddy [1935] I.R. 397; 70 I.L.T.R. 28 13
Nguyen v. Nguyen (No. 1) (1990) 169 C.L.R. 245; 64 A.L.J.R. 222 62
Nguyen v. Nguyen (No. 2) [1992] 1 Qd. R. 405 63
Noone v. Minister for Finance [1964] I.R. 63 54
Nunan v. Southern Railway Co [1924] 1 K.B. 223; 93 L.J.K.B. 140;
   130 L.T. 131; 40 T.L.R. 21 59

O'Brien v. Ulster Bank Ltd, unreported, High Court,
   December 21, 1993 30
O'Brien v. Waterford County Council [1926] I.R. 1 72
O'Connell v. Jackson [1972] 1 Q.B. 270; [1971] 3 W.L.R. 463; [1971]
   3 All E.R. 129 41
O'Connor v. McDonnell, unreported, High Court, June 30, 1970 67
O'Hanlon v. Electricity Supply Board [1969] I.R. 75; 105 I.L.T.R. 25 43
O'Loughlin v. Teeling [1988] I.L.R.M. 617 83
O'Neill v. Ryanair Ltd (No. 2) [1992] 1 I.R. 160 15
O'Sullivan v. Córas Iompair Éireann [1978] I.R. 409 61
O'Sullivan v. Dwyer [1971] I.R. 275 .... 41, 54

Parry v. Cleaver [1970] A.C. 1; [1969] 2 W.L.R. 821; [1969]
   1 All E.R. 555 80
Parsons v. BNM Laboratories Ltd [1964] 1 Q.B. 95; [1963]
   2 W.L.R. 1273; [1963] 2 All E.R. 658 80
Patterson v. Murphy [1978] I.L.R.M. 85 24
Payne v. Railway Executive [1952] 1 K.B. 26; [1951] 2 All E.R. 910 80
Pitts v. Hunt [1991] 1 Q.B. 24; [1990] 3 W.L.R. 542; [1990]
   3 All E.R. 344 .... 42, 68
Plant v. Chadwick (1986) 5 B.C.L.R. (2d) 305; [1986] 6 W.W.R. 131 63
Power v. Bedford Motor Co Ltd [1959] I.R. 391; 94 I.L.T.R. 71 .... 12, 13
Preston v. Dowell (1987) 45 S.A.S.R. 111 68

Progress and Properties Ltd v. Craft (1976) 135 C.L.R. 651;
    51 A.L.J.R. 184 68
Public Trustee v. Zoanetti (1945) 70 C.L.R. 266 62
Pym v. Great Northern Railway Co (1863) 4 B. & S. 396; 32 L.J.Q.B.
    377; 8 L.T. 734 65

Quirke v. O'Shea [1992] I.L.R.M. 286 33

Rawlinson v. Babcock & Wilcox Ltd [1967] 1 W.L.R. 481; [1966]
    3 All E.R. 882 63
Read & Great Eastern Railway Co (1868) L.R. 3 Q.B. 555; 37
    L.J.Q.B. 278; 18 L.T. 822 59
Reamsbottom v. Raftery [1991] 1 I.R. 531 48
Redpath v. Belfast and County Down Railway [1947] N.I. 167 81
Regan v. Irish Automobile Club Ltd [1990] 1 I.R. 278 43
Roe v. Minister for Health [1954] 2 Q.B. 66; [1954] 2 W.L.R. 915;
    [1954] 2 All E.R. 131 12
Rookes v. Barnard [1964] A.C. 1129; [1964] 2 W.L.R. 269; [1964]
    1 All E.R. 367 8
Russell v. The Men Dwelling in the County of Devon (1788) 2 T.R. 667;
    100 E.R. 339 72
Ryan v. Ireland [1989] I.L.R.M. 544 43

Sea-Land Services Inc. v. Gandet (1974) 414 U.S. 573 59
Seymour v. British Paints (Australia) Pty Ltd [1967] Qd. R. 227 62
SFL Engineering Ltd v. Smyth Cladding Systems Ltd, unreported, High
    Court, May 9, 1997 .... 30, 32
Shanley v. Casey [1967] I.R. 338 .... 75, 76
Shaw v. Sloan [1982] N.I. 393 49
Skelding v. Skelding (1992) 98 D.L.R. (4th) 219 63
Smith v. Jenkins (1970) 119 C.L.R. 397; 44 A.L.J.R. 78 67
Smith v. Streatfield [1913] 3 K.B. 704; 82 L.J.K.B. 1237; 109 L.T. 173;
    29 T.L.R. 707 13
Smoker v. London Fire and Civil Defence Authority [1991] 2 A.C. 502;
    [1991] 2 W.L.R. 1052; [1991] 2 All E.R. 449; [1991] I.C.R. 449 80
Spittle v. Bunney [1988] 1 W.L.R. 847; [1988] 3 All E.R. 1031 63
St Laurence's Hospital, Board of Governors of v. Staunton [1990]
    2 I.R. 31 30
Stanley v. Saddique [1992] 1 Q.B. 1; [1991] 2 W.L.R. 459; [1991]
    1 All E.R. 529 63
State (Hayes) v. Criminal Injuries Compensation Tribunal [1982]
    I.L.R.M. 210 65
State (Sheehan) v. Government of Ireland [1987] I.R. 550 72
Staunton v. Toyota (Ireland) Ltd, unreported, High Court, April 15,
    1988 .... 23, 24, 32, 34
Stonehouse v. Gamble (1983) 44 B.C.L.R. 375; 24 C.C.L.T. 133 63
Summers v. Tice (1948) 5 A.L.R. 2d 91 13

Sun Life Assurance Co of Canada v. Dalrymple (1965) 50 D.L.R.
(2d) 217 13

Thomas v. Quartermaine (1887) 18 Q.B.D. 685; 56 L.J.Q.B. 340;
57 L.T. 537 43
Tierney v. Fintan Sweeney Ltd, unreported, High Court,
October 18, 1995 32

Urquhart and Hatt, Re (1982) 132 D.L.R. (3d) 685 37

Van Gervan v. Fenton (1992) 175 C.L.R. 327; 66 A.L.J.R. 828 62
Van Keep v. Surface Dressing Contractors Ltd, unreported,
High Court, June 11, 1993 83
Van Win Pty Ltd v. Eleventh Mirontron Pty Ltd [1986] V.R. 484 37
Vana v. Tosta (1968) 66 D.L.R. (2d) 97 61

Walker v. Great Northern Railway Co (1891) 28 L.R.I.R. 69 70
Ward v. McMaster [1985] I.R. 29 24
Ward v. O'Callaghan, unreported, High Court, February 2, 1998 33
Waters v. Cruikshank [1967] I.R. 378; 103 I.L.T.R. 129 58
Webb v. The State of South Australia (1982) 56 A.L.J.R. 912 73
Wells v. McBrine (1988) 54 D.L.R. (4th) 708 41
Whitter v. DeSousa (1989) 16 A.W.C.S. (3d) 176 63
Wickberg v. Patterson (1997) 145 D.L.R. (4th) 263 40
Williams v. Mersey Docks and Harbour Board [1905] 1 K.B. 804 59
Williams v. Tom Duffy & Co. UD 687/1986 8
Wilson v. McGrath, unreported, High Court, January 17, 1996 41
Wilson v. Minister for Finance [1944] I.R. 142 15
Winnik v. Dick 1984 S.L.T. 185 68
Woodman Matheson & Co Ltd v. Brennan (1941) 75 I.L.T.R. 34 81
Wrightcel (New Zealand) Ltd v. Felvin Suppliers and Distributors Ltd
[1975] N.Z.L.R. 50 38

CIVIL LIABILITY ACT 1961

(1961 No. 12)

ARRANGEMENT OF SECTIONS

PART I

PRELIMINARY AND GENERAL

SECT.
1. Short title and collective citation.
2. Interpretation generally.
3. Adaptation of references to repealed Acts.
4. Savings.
5. Repeals.

PART II

SURVIVAL OF CERTAIN CAUSES OF ACTION ON DEATH

6. Definition (Part II).
7. Survival of certain causes of action vested in deceased person.
8. Survival of certain causes of action subsisting against deceased person.
9. Time limit in respect of causes of action which survive against estate of deceased person.
10. Insolvency of estate against which proceedings are maintainable.

PART III

CONCURRENT FAULT

11. Persons who are concurrent wrongdoers.
12. Extent of liability.
13. Joinder of defendants.
14. Judgments to be several.
15. Judgment by default.
16. Discharge and estoppel by satisfaction.
17. Release of, or accord with, one wrongdoer.
18. Judgment against one wrongdoer.
19. Judgment in favour of one alleged wrongdoer.
20. Limitation of actions against one of concurrent wrongdoers.
21. Contribution in respect of damages.
22. Contribution claimed by settling tortfeasor.
23. Enforcement of judgment for contribution.
24. Contribution in respect of costs.
25. One wrongdoer omitted from claim for contribution; contribution in respect of contribution.
26. Contribution where property is restored to its owner.
27. Procedure for claiming contribution.

1

28. Distribution of loss on failure to obtain satisfaction.
29. Estoppel when contribution is claimed.
30. Legal incidents of claim for contribution.
31. Limitation of actions for contribution.
32. Evidence and appeals.
33. Contribution to be regarded as damages.
34. Apportionment of liability in case of contributory negligence.
35. Identifications.
36. Set-off of claims.
37. Estoppel in case of contributory negligence.
38. Liability of concurrent wrongdoers where plaintiff guilty of contributory negligence.
39. Bankruptcy of one wrongdoer.
40. Special findings.
41. Courts of limited jurisdiction.
42. Costs in cases of contributory negligence.
43. Application for breaches of strict duty.
44. One-sided periods of limitation.
45. Restitution.
46. Maritime cases.

PART IV

FATAL INJURIES

47. Definitions.
48. Action where death caused by wrongful act, neglect or default.
49. Damages.
50. Sums not to be taken into account in assessing damages.
51. Adaptation of references to Fatal Accidents Acts 1846 to 1908.

PART V

AMENDMENTS OF THE WORKMEN'S COMPENSATION ACTS 1934 TO 1955

52–54. [Repealed].

PART VI

AMENDMENT OF TBE AIR NAVIGATION AND TRANSPORT ACT 1936

55. Re-enactment, with amendments, of section 18 of the Act of 1936.

PART VII

MISCELLANEOUS

56. Abolition of last opportunity rule.
57. Abolition of defences.
58. Wrongs to unborn child.
59. Liability of Minister for Finance for negligent use of mechanically propelled vehicle.

60. Liability of road authority for failure to maintain public road.
61. Proof of claims for damages or contribution in bankruptcy.
62. Application of moneys payable under certain policies of insurance.
63. Costs in certain actions in which the plaintiff is an infant.
    Schedule.

An Act to reform the law relating to civil liability, providing in particular for the survival of causes of action on death, for proceedings against and contribution between concurrent wrongdoers and for liability in cases of contributory negligence, to provide for damages for the benefit of the dependants of any person fatally injured by the wrongful act, neglect or default of another, and to provide for other matters connected with the foregoing. [17*th August,* 1961]

INTRODUCTION AND GENERAL NOTE

The Civil Liability Act 1961, which was designed to reform the law as to civil liability, became law on August 17, 1961. Its purpose is fourfold: first, it amends and consolidates the law relating to the survival of causes of action on death; secondly, it amends and declares the law concerning concurrent fault; thirdly, it re-enacts, in the light of the foregoing, the statutory provisions in regard to damages for the benefit of the dependants of persons fatally injured; and, finally, it makes certain miscellaneous amendments in the law relating to wrongdoing. The Act was amended and extended by the Civil Liability (Amendment) Act 1964 and by the Civil Liability (Amendment) Act 1996.

Kutner, writing in (1985) 63 Can. Bar Rev. 1 at 3, described the 1961 Act as being a statute of "unique detail and complexity"; a fact which led Murnaghan J., speaking extra judicially (SYS Lecture No. 36, November 3, 1968), to say that the Act appeared to have been constructed "on an academic rather than a practical foundation". This is undoubtedly because, with certain variations, the Act is essentially that drafted by Dr Glanville Williams in *Joint Torts and Contributory Negligence* (1954) (hereafter referred to as *JTCN*). This was specifically acknowledged by Charles Haughey T.D. (Vol. 188 *Dáil Debates* cols. 1592 and 1597), who went on to say that Dr Glanville Williams at an early stage was kind enough to offer the Department of Justice any help and had placed at the Department's disposal "the results of his scholarship and research not alone in regard to concurrent fault but also in regard to problems in connection with the survival of causes of action on death." The Act, therefore, according to Professors McMahon and Binchy in *Irish Law of Torts* (2nd ed., 1990), p. 351, "has all the advantages of a thorough and incisive analysis by a legal expert of world renown who took full account of the strengths and weaknesses of statutory reforms in other jurisdictions." See also Fleming in (1976) 64 Calif. L. Rev. 239, who makes frequent reference to the "sophisticated Irish statute". Moreover, during the Second Stage debate, John A. Costello T.D. said he knew from personal experience that "a great deal of hard work, research, legal erudition and industry of a very high calibre" had gone into the preparation and drafting of the Act (Vol. 188 *Dáil Debates* cols. 1605–5). Despite this, the draftsmanship in the Act was condemned, on more than one occasion, by Murnaghan J. as being "inadequate". See for instance *Gillespie v. Fitzpatrick (No. 2)*, unreported, High Court, April 27, 1970 at 21 of the judgment and *Lynch v. Lynch*, unreported, High Court, November 24, 1976 where it was described, at 2, as "a very difficult and sometimes impossible Act to construe". More recently McCarthy J., in *Murphy v. J. Donohoe Ltd.* [1992] I.L.R.M. 378 at 394, commented that the Act's provenance meant that the wording of some sections was not as it would have been if drafted from the start by a parliamentary draftsman.

Part II of the 1961 Act amends and consolidates the law relating to the survival of causes of action on death. At common law the maxim *actio personalis moritur cum persona* applied in the sphere of tort. Claims in debt or for breach of contract or in respect of bonds, deeds or covenants were unaffected by the death of either party. Most actions of tort, however, died with the person, whether the deceased person was the injured person or the wrongdoer. Certain statutory exceptions to the rule were contained in two ancient statutes of 1285 and 1330, applied to Ireland by Poynings' Law in 1495 and in section 31 of the Debtors (Ireland) Act 1840. These enactments gave the personal representative the same right of action as the deceased would have had if alive in respect of trespass or injury to the real or personal estate of the deceased committed in his lifetime, although in the case of realty, the injury had to have been committed within six months before the death and the action had to have been brought within one year after the death. Other exceptions could be found in section 23 of the Air Navigation and Transport Act 1936, section 6 of the Fatal Injuries Act 1956 and section 17 of the Road Traffic Act 1961. All these provisions were repealed by the 1961 Act.

Part III of the 1961 Act, which itself is divided into four chapters, amends, clarifies and restates the law concerning concurrent fault, specifically the liability of concurrent wrong-doers, contribution between concurrent wrongdoers and contributory negligence. The object of this Part was, *per* Walsh J. in *Gilmore v. Windle* [1967] I.R. 323 at 332, "to simplify litigation and to avoid multiplicity of actions" so as to enable all issues arising out of a particular incident or transaction to be determined by the one court at one time: see also Finlay C.J. in *International Commercial Bank plc v. Insurance Corporation of Ireland* [1989] I.L.R.M. 788 at 799–800 and *Kelly v. Governors of St. Laurence's Hospital* [1989] I.L.R.M. 877 at 879. The fundamental purpose of the 'contribution' provisions is to achieve an equitable division among the wrongdoers of the financial burden of liability to the victim. Prior to the 1961 Act, the law, particularly in relation to contributory negligence, had become bedeviled with a bewildering array of concepts such as the "last opportunity rule" and "the third question". These concepts had been evolved by the common law in an attempt to mitigate the harshness of the rule that the contributory negligence of the plaintiff defeated his claim.

Part IV of the 1961 Act re-enacts and amends the relevant provisions of the Fatal Injuries Act 1956 which itself consolidated and amended the Fatal Accidents Acts 1846–1908. At common law the death of a person could not be complained of as an injury: see *Baker v. Bolton* (1808)1 Camp. 493. This resulted in injustice particularly to dependants of persons wrongfully killed by another. This injustice and hardship was recognised by the legislature and was mitigated in 1846 by Lord Campbell's Act (9 & 10 Vic., c. 93). On *Baker v. Bolton* see Malone, "The Genesis of Wrongful Death" (1965)17 Stanford L. Rev. 1043 and on whether there is an action for wrongful death "at Irish common law" see White, *Irish Law of Damages* (1989), pp. 285–304. The 1961 Act also makes provision for a limited award of damages, in the nature of solatium, for the dependants' mental distress resulting from the death.

PART I

PRELIMINARY AND GENERAL

Short title and collective citation

1.—(1) This Act may be cited as the Civil Liability Act 1961.

(2) The Air Navigation and Transport Acts 1936 to 1959, and Part VI of this Act may be cited together as the Air Navigation and Transport Acts 1936 to 1961.

GENERAL NOTE

Section 7(2) of the Civil Liability (Amendment) Act 1964 provides that the two Acts may be cited together as the Civil Liability Acts 1961 and 1964.

Interpretation generally

2.—(1) In this Act, save where the context otherwise requires—

"the Act of 1936" means the Air Navigation and Transport Act 1936;

"the Statute of Limitations" means the Statute of Limitations 1957;

"act" includes default or other omission;

"action" includes counterclaim and proceedings by way of arbitration;

"any other limitation enactment" includes sections 31, 46 and 48;

"bankrupt" includes an arranging debtor;

"bankruptcy" includes an arrangement under an order of the court for protection;

"concurrent wrongs" means wrongs committed by persons in respect of which they are concurrent wrongdoers;

"contract" means a contract under seal or by parol;

"contributor" means a person who is liable or alleged to be liable to make contribution;

"court" means, in relation to any claim, the court or arbitrator by or before whom the claim falls to be determined;

"damage" includes loss of property, loss of life and personal injury;

"damages", except in Part IV, includes compensation for breach of trust;

"defendant", includes defendant to a counterclaim;

"injured person" means a person against whom a wrong is committed;

"liable" refers to legal liability whether or not enforceable by action;

"negligence" includes breach of statutory duty;

"personal injury includes any disease and any impairment of a person's physical or mental condition, and "injured" shall be construed accordingly;

"plaintiff" includes a defendant counterclaiming and a defendant claiming against a co-defendant by notice or otherwise;

"third-party" includes fourth party and subsequent party;

"wrong" means a tort, breach of contract or breach of trust, whether the act is committed by the person to whom the wrong is attributed or by one for whose acts he is responsible, and whether or not the act is also a crime, and whether or not the wrong is intentional;

"wrong of the defendant" includes, where the defendant is a personal representative, a wrong of the deceased for which the defendant is liable as personal representative;

"wrongdoer" means a person who commits or is otherwise responsible for a wrong.

(2) Any reference in this Act to any other enactment shall be construed as a reference to that enactment as amended or applied by any subsequent enactment, including this Act.

GENERAL NOTE

"Arranging debtor": section 3 of the Bankruptcy Act 1988 defines this term as meaning "a debtor who has been granted an order for protection under Part IV [of the 1988 Act]".

"The Statute of Limitations": the Statute of 1957 was amended by the Statute of Limitations (Amendment) Act 1991.

"Wrong": the Rules of the Superior Courts 1986, Ord. 19, r. 5(1), provide that:

> in all cases alleging a wrong within the meaning of the Civil Liability Acts 1961 and 1964, particulars of such wrong, any personal injuries suffered and any items of special damage shall be set out in the statement of claim or counterclaim and particulars of any contributory negligence shall be set out in the defence.

Section 21(4)(a) of the Control of Dogs Act 1986 provides that any damage or injury for which a person is made liable under section 21 shall be deemed to be attributable to a wrong within the meaning of the 1961 Act and the provisions of that Act shall apply accordingly.

Adaptation of references to repealed Acts

3.—A reference in any enactment to any Act repealed by this Act shall be construed as a reference to this Act.

Savings

4.—(1) Nothing in this Act shall have effect in relation to any cause of action which accrued before the passing of this Act.

(2) Nothing in this Act shall—

    (a) render enforceable any agreement for indemnity which would not have been enforceable if this Act had not been passed, or

    (b) affect the power of the court to stay proceedings that are an abuse of the process of the court.

Repeals

5.—The enactments mentioned in the Schedule are hereby repealed to the extent specified in column (3); except in respect of cases saved by section 4.

GENERAL NOTE

The Schedule is reproduced at page 77 *infra*.

PART II

SURVIVAL OF CERTAIN CAUSES OF ACTION ON DEATH

Preliminary

Definition (Part II)

6.—In this Part "excepted cause of action" means—
  (a) a cause of action for breach of promise to marry or for defamation or for seduction or for inducing one spouse to leave or remain apart from the other or for criminal conversation, or
  (b) any claim for compensation under the Workmen's Compensation Act 1934.

GENERAL NOTE

Actions for criminal conversation and for inducing one spouse to leave or remain apart from the other were abolished by section 1(1) of the Family Law Act 1981. Actions for breach of promise to marry were abolished by section 2(1) of the Family Law Act 1981. By virtue of section 40 of the Social Welfare (Occupational Injuries) Act 1966 (as amended by the Social Welfare (Consolidation) Act 1981) the Workmen's Compensation Acts 1934–1955 were repealed, thus rendering section 6(b) redundant for all practical purposes. Therefore the only operative 'excepted causes of action' are defamation and seduction.

For a general overview of the law of defamation see McDonald, *Irish Law of Defamation* (2nd ed., 1989); Boyle and McGonagle, *A Report on Press Freedom and Libel* (National Newspapers of Ireland, 1988) and the Law Reform Commission, *Report on the Civil Law of Defamation* (LRC 38–1991). With regard to seduction see Shatter, *Family Law In the Republic of Ireland* (4th ed., 1997), pp. 261–266; Law Reform Commission Working Paper No. 6, *The Law Relating to Seduction and the Enticement and Harbouring of a Child* (1979). In the Law Reform Commission, *First Report on Family Law* (1981), it was recommended that the existing action for seduction of a child be abolished and, replaced, by a single family action for seduction. This recommendation was trenchantly criticised by Shatter, *op. cit.*, p. 265.

Causes of Action vested in Deceased Person

Survival of certain causes of action vested in deceased person

7.—(1) On the death of a person on or after the date of the passing of this Act all causes of action (other than excepted causes of action) vested in him shall survive for the benefit of his estate.

(2) Where, by virtue of subsection (1) of this section, a cause of action survives for the benefit of the estate of a deceased person, the damages recoverable for the benefit of the estate of that person shall not include exemplary damages, or damages for any pain or suffering or personal injury or for loss or diminution of expectation of life or happiness.

(3) Where—
  (a) a cause of action survives by virtue of subsection (1) of this section for the benefit of the estate of a deceased person, and
  (b) the death of such person has been caused by the circumstances which gave rise to such cause of action,

the damages recoverable for the benefit of his estate shall be calculated without reference to any loss or gain to his estate consequent on his death, except that a sum in respect of funeral expenses may be included.

(4) The rights conferred by this section for the benefit of the estate of a deceased person are in addition to the rights conferred on the dependants of deceased persons by Part III of the Act of 1936 and Part IV of this Act.

GENERAL NOTE

This section makes provision for the survival of causes of action which are vested in the deceased person for the benefit of his or her estate (as opposed to actions which enure for the benefit of his or her estate). The effect of subsection (1) is that a cause of action vested in a person before his or her death is, on death, transmitted to the deceased's estate and may be pursued by the personal representatives on behalf of the estate.

The fact that a deceased has brought a personal injury action which was settled or sued to judgment precludes the bringing of a fatal accidents claim on his or her death: *per* Lavan J., *Mahon v. Burke* [1991] 2 I.R. 495 at 500.

The Employment Appeals Tribunal has held that a claim under the Unfair Dismissals Act 1977 comes within the ambit of this section: *Williams v. Tom Duffy & Co.*, UD 687/1986 (reproduced in Madden and Kerr, *Unfair Dismissal: Cases and Commentary* (2nd ed.), p.60). Note that section 1 of the 1977 Act defines "employee" as including, "in the case of the death of the employee concerned at any time following the dismissal, his personal representative".

Subsection (2) excludes the possibility of recovery of exemplary damages for the benefit of the estate. On the question of exemplary damages see *Conway v. Irish National Teachers' Organisation* [1991] 2 I.R. 305, where the restrictions imposed by the House of Lords in *Rookes v. Barnard* [1964] A.C. 1129 on the right to recover such damages were not adopted. In *Conway*, Griffin J. said that exemplary damages might be awarded where there had been wilful and conscious wrongdoing in contumelious disregard of another's rights (at 323). The object in awarding such damages was to punish the wrongdoer for his outrageous conduct, to deter him and others from any such conduct in the future and to mark the court's (or the jury's) detestation and disapproval of that conduct. See also the *dicta* of O'Flaherty J. in *McIntyre v. Lewis* [1991] 1 I.R. 121 at 140–141.

The Irish law on exemplary damages is thoroughly reviewed in Chapter 7 of the Law Reform Commission's *Consultation Paper on Aggravated, Exemplary and Restitutionary Damages* (April 1998). The Commission, in paragraph 7.50, expressed the view that the exclusion of exemplary damages awards to the estate of a deceased person appeared to be "at odds" with the nature of these damages. See further, the Commission's recommendations at paragraphs 9.91 and 9.92, to the effect that section 7 should be amended to allow for the recovery of exemplary damages where a cause of action survives for the benefit of the estate of a deceased person.

While subsection (2) expressly excludes the possibility of recovery for damages for pain and suffering, personal injury or loss, or diminution of expectation of life or happiness, it does not exclude the possibility of recovery of damages representing loss of earnings during the "lost years" of the deceased's expected life span: see *Gammell v. Wilson* [1982] A.C. 27. As is pointed out in Salmond and Heuston, *The Law of Torts* (21st ed., 1996), p. 532, this opens up the possibility of substantial claims for damages against wrongdoers if deceased persons have left their estate to persons other than their dependants.

Subsection (3) provides that, in an action brought on behalf of a deceased's estate in respect of a wrong which has occasioned the death of the deceased, losses and gains to the estate consequent on the death cannot be taken into account. Therefore, as White points out in *Irish Law of Damages* (1989), p. 441, the damages cannot be increased by sums representing taxes paid by the estate on the death or reduced on account of sums received by the estate under an insurance policy. A sum in respect of funeral expenses, however, may be included.

Subsection (4) expressly provides that the action on behalf of the estate under subsection (1) is completely unaffected by recovery of damages in a wrongful death action brought by the deceased's dependants under Part IV of the Act. The converse, however, is not the case and the damages recoverable in a wrongful death action may be affected by the amount received in an action on behalf of the estate. As can be seen from the annotation to section 49 (page 62 *infra*), the courts, in assessing the loss of a dependency, have always had regard to the benefits accruing to the dependants from the deceased's estate.

Note that under section 48 of the Succession Act 1965, the personal representatives of a deceased person may sue in respect of all causes of action which by virtue of Part II of the Civil Liability Act 1961 survive for the benefit of the estate of the deceased. Note also that section 4 of the Statute of Limitations (Amendment) Act 1991 provides that, if an injured person to whom section 3 of the 1991 Act applies dies before the expiration of three years from the date on which the cause of action accrued or the "date of knowledge" (if later) of the person injured, any cause of action to which that section applies by virtue of section 7 of the 1961 Act may be brought at any time before the expiration of three years from:

    (a)   the date of death, or

    (b)   the date of the personal representative's knowledge,

whichever is the later. Section 2 of the 1991 Act sets out what is meant by a person's "date of knowledge". On the 1991 Act generally, see Kerr, *The Statute of Limitations (Amendment) Act 1991* (1991 Irish Current Law Statutes Annotated, Round Hall Sweet & Maxwell).

Causes of Action subsisting against Deceased Persons

Survival of certain causes of action subsisting against deceased person

8.—(1) On the death of a person on or after the date of the passing of this Act all causes of action (other than excepted causes of action) subsisting against him shall survive against his estate.

(2) Where damage has been suffered by reason of any act in respect of which a cause of action would have subsisted against any person if he had not died before or at the same time as the damage was suffered, there shall be deemed, for the purposes of subsection (1) of this section, to have been subsisting against him before his death such cause of action in respect of that act as would have subsisted if he had died after the damage was suffered.

GENERAL NOTE

This section provides for causes of action subsisting against a deceased person. The Employment Appeals Tribunal has accepted that proceedings under the Unfair Dismissals Act 1977 constitute an action for the purposes of section 8: see *Hutton v. Philippi* [1982] I.L.R.M. 578. The section imposes no restriction on the type of damages that may be recovered against the estate of the deceased. A cause of action which survives against the estate of a deceased person must be one subsisting at the date of his death: see Barron J. in *Bank of Ireland v. O'Keeffe*, unreported, High Court, December 3, 1986.

Subsection (2) covers the case where the wrongdoer dies before or at the same time as the damage is suffered.

Time limit in respect of causes of action which survive against estate of deceased person

9.—(1) In this section "the relevant period" means the period of limitation prescribed by the Statute of Limitations or any other limitation enactment.

(2) No proceedings shall be maintainable in respect of any cause of action whatsoever which has survived against the estate of a deceased person unless

either—

(a) proceedings against him in respect of that cause of action were commenced within the relevant period and were pending at the date of his death, and

(b) proceedings are commenced in respect of that cause of action within the relevant period or within the period of two years after his death, whichever period first expires.

GENERAL NOTE

Section 9 was inserted at Committee Stage in the Dáil Debates. The section is applicable only to actions against the estate of a deceased and not to actions taken by personal representatives for the benefit of the estate. In the latter case, the normal limitation periods imposed by the Statutes of Limitations 1957 and 1991 apply, see Brady and Kerr, *The Limitation of Actions in the Republic of Ireland* (2nd ed., 1994). Section 7(3) of the Liability for Defective Products Act 1991 provides that section 9 shall not apply to an action for the recovery of damages under that Act and section 281(3A) of the Social Welfare (Consolidation) Act 1993 (inserted by section 41 of the Social Welfare Act 1996) provides that section 9 shall not apply to an action for the recovery of a debt due to the Minister for Social, Community and Family Affairs or to the State under that Act.

Although it was not necessary for him to deal with the point in any great depth, Barron J., in *Bank of Ireland v. O'Keeffe*, unreported, High Court, December 3, 1986, said that it seemed quite clear that the relevant period referred to in subsection (1) "includes not only the basic period of limitation laid down by the Statute but also the extension of such basic period by reason of such matters as acknowledgements in writing, mistake etc."

The validity of section 9(2)(b) was unsuccessfully challenged in *Moynihan v. Greensmyth* [1977] I.R. 55. There, a sixteen-year old girl was injured on August 6, 1966, while travelling as a passenger in a vehicle driven by the defendant, who was killed in the accident. Proceedings were instituted on behalf of the plaintiff on August 5, 1969, which would have been within the normal limitation period prescribed by the Statute of Limitations 1957. Section 11(2)(b) of the 1957 Act provides that, in respect of a claim for personal injuries, an action shall not be brought after three years from the date on which the cause of action accrued; and in respect of a person labouring under a disability — such as minority — section 49 provides that the action may be brought at any time before the expiration of three years from the date when the person ceased to be under the disability. Thus, had the defendant been still alive, the plaintiff's cause of action would not have been barred until 1974. Nevertheless, it was pleaded that the plaintiff's claim was statute barred by virtue of the provisions of section 9 of the Civil Liability Act 1961. The plaintiff contended that section 9(2)(b) was invalid having regard to the provisions of Article 40.3.2° of the Constitution. This claim was rejected by Murnaghan J., whose decision was upheld by the Supreme Court; the Court holding that there was no unjust attack on the alleged property rights of the infant plaintiff because the State had to strike a balance between those alleged property rights and the rights of other persons interested in the early completion of the administration of the deceased's estate. The plaintiff's claim, therefore, was statute barred not having been instituted within two years after the defendant's death.

Insolvency of estate against which proceedings are maintainable

10.—In the event of the insolvency of an estate against which proceedings are maintainable, any liability in respect of the cause of action in respect of which the proceedings are maintainable shall be deemed to be a debt provable in the administration of the estate, notwithstanding that it is a demand in the nature of unliquidated damages arising otherwise than by a contract or promise.

GENERAL NOTE

This section, which is of general application and applies irrespective of whether the cause of action arises at common law or by virtue of section 8, makes provision for cases where the deceased person's estate against which proceedings are being taken is insolvent. The liability is to be a debt provable in the administration of the estate, but it will not of itself support a bankruptcy petition. The section is in similar terms to section 1(6) of the English Law Reform (Miscellaneous Provisions) Act 1934.

PART III

CONCURRENT FAULT

GENERAL NOTE

Section 8 of the Liability for Defective Products Act 1991 provides that, where two or more persons are liable by virtue of the 1991 Act for the same damage, they shall be liable jointly and severally as concurrent wrongdoers within the meaning of this Part of the 1961 Act.

CHAPTER I

Liability of Concurrent Wrongdoers

Persons who are concurrent wrongdoers

11.—(1) For the purpose of this Part, two or more persons are concurrent wrongdoers when both or all are wrongdoers and are responsible to a third person (in this Part called the injured person or the plaintiff) for the same damage, whether or not judgment has been recovered against some or all of them.

(2) Without prejudice to the generality of subsection (1) of this section—

    (a) persons may become concurrent wrongdoers as a result of vicarious liability of one for another, breach of joint duty, conspiracy, concerted action to a common end or independent acts causing the same damage;

    (b) the wrong on the part of one or both may be a tort, breach of contract or breach of trust, or any combination of them;

    (c) it is immaterial whether the acts constituting concurrent wrongs are contemporaneous or successive.

(3) Where two or more persons are at fault and one or more of them is or are responsible for damage while the other or others is or are free from causal responsibility, but it is not possible to establish which is the case, such two or more persons shall be deemed to be concurrent wrongdoers in respect of the damage.

(4) Where there is a joint libel in circumstances normally protected by the defences of qualified privilege or fair comment upon a matter of public interest, the malice of one person shall not defeat the defence for the other, unless that other is vicariously liable for the malice of the first.

(5) Where the same or substantially the same libel or slander or injurious falsehood is published by different persons, the court shall take into consideration the extent to which it is probable that the statement in question was published directly or indirectly to the same persons, and to that extent may find the wrongdoers to be concurrent wrongdoers.

(6) For the purpose of any enactment referring to a specific tort, an action for a conspiracy to commit that tort shall be deemed to be an action for that tort.

GENERAL NOTE

This section defines "concurrent wrongdoers" and abolishes the distinction between joint and several tortfeasors. The difference between joint tortfeasors and several tortfeasors was well put by Fleming, *The Law of Torts* (8th ed., 1992), p. 255, in that the former are responsible for the same tort, whereas the latter are responsible only for the same damage. The section was considered by Hamilton J. (as he then was) in *Lynch v. Beale*, unreported, High Court, November 23, 1974, where a building owner sued his architect, his main contractor and his nominated subcontractor for loss sustained by him as a result of the negligence and breach of contract of the three named defendants in the construction of a hotel premises. The premises had collapsed due to two main factors, *i.e.* the subsidence of the foundations in a corner of the building and inadequate design in the first floor of the building. The nominated subcontractor argued, and it was submitted on behalf of the architect, that, as there were two separate and distinct causes for the structural defects, the defendants were not "concurrent wrongdoers" and that, if there was any liability on behalf of any of the defendants, such liability should be limited to the actual loss resulting from the particular wrong committed by any defendant. Hamilton J. rejected this contention saying:

> The damage claimed in this case against all the defendants is the same damage, viz: the loss sustained by him as a result of the internal collapse of the hotel and the subsidence thereof and the Court is satisfied that the defendants herein are "concurrent wrongdoers" as defined in the Civil Liability Act 1961.

It is clear, therefore, that in determining whether parties are to be regarded as concurrent wrongdoers, primary emphasis is to be placed on the damage caused and not on the role played by each of the defendants, provided each contributed to causation.

Subsection (3) was designed to provide for the situation where a person has sustained damage as a result of the wrong of one or more persons but where it is not possible to ascertain which person was responsible. At common law it was established that, in respect of several concurrent (but not joint) tortfeasors, if at the end of the case the plaintiff had proved that he was negligently injured by either the first-named defendant or the second-named defendant, but was unable to establish which of the two caused the injury, his action must fail against both (see Kingsmill Moore J. in *Power v. Bedford Motor Co. Ltd* [1959] I.R. 391 at 420) unless one was vicariously liable for the other.

In Canada and California, the rule had been relaxed where two or more persons act negligently to the plaintiff but there is no proof aside from the fact that his or her injury was caused by one or other of them alone. In *Cook v. Lewis* [1952] 1 D.L.R. 1 (on which see Glanville Williams (1953) 31 Can. Bar Rev. 315 and Hogan (1961) 24 M.L.R. 331) and *Summers v. Tice* (1948) 5 A.L.R. 2d 91, the Supreme Courts of Canada and California respectively held that, in such a case, the evidential burden was cast on each to exculpate himself or herself. See also *obiter* Denning L.J. in *Roe v. Minister for Health* [1954] 2 Q.B. 66 at 82, and Salmond and Heuston, *The Law of Torts* (21st ed., 1996), p.242.

That this subsection is not free from interpretative difficulty has been noted by Murnaghan J., who, speaking extra-judicially (SYS Lecture No. 36, November 3, 1968), interpreted "fault" as meaning "responsibility for something wrong", that is, the injuries to the plaintiff. He illustrated the difficulties by referring to *Boles v. O'Connor*, unreported, High Court, February 21, 1964. In this case, a car was travelling along its correct side of the road when it collided with a telegraph pole. As a result the vehicle came to a stationary position across and blocking the left hand side of the road — its correct side. Another vehicle, which had been travelling behind the first vehicle, crashed into the side of the first vehicle. Later a passenger in the first vehicle was found lying out of the passenger door with his head touching the road. He had sustained serious injuries from which he died. Murnaghan J., said he would have been in no difficulty in finding sufficient evidence of negligence on the part of both drivers; he nevertheless found difficulty in determining whether both drivers had been at fault in the sense that they were both responsible for the injuries of the deceased. He thought that the facts were open to at least two constructions: either the passenger sustained his injuries as a result of the first collision, in which case the driver of the second vehicle was free from "causal responsibility" or both collisions contributed to the seriousness of the injuries sustained by the deceased. In this case both drivers would have been at fault.

It is arguable that the meaning attributed by Murnaghan J., to the word "fault" as used in subsection (3) is not entirely accurate. Although the learned judge equated "fault" with causal responsibility, the subsection is clearly designed to deem a person who is free from causal responsibility to be a concurrent wrongdoer, provided he is at fault. Exactly what the meaning is remains to be considered by the courts, but its most likely connotation is lack of care towards the plaintiff. Despite the observations of Kingsmill Moore J. in *Power v. Bedford Motor Co. Ltd*, it is submitted that the words of the Supreme Court of California in *Summers v. Tice* (1948) 5 A.L.R. at 96 are apposite:

> When we consider the relative position of the parties and the results that would flow if the plaintiff was required to pin the injury on one of the defendants only, a requirement that the burden of proof on that subject be shifted to the defendants becomes manifest. They are both wrongdoers — both negligent towards the plaintiff. They brought about a situation where the negligence of one of them injured the plaintiff, hence it should rest with them each to absolve himself if he can. The injured party has been placed by the defendants in the unfair position of pointing to which defendant caused the harm. If one can escape the other may also and the plaintiff is remediless. Ordinarily defendants are in a far better position to offer evidence to determine which one caused the injury.

The effect of subsection (4) is to treat the position of each defendant in a defamation action separately for the purposes of determining whether the defences of qualified privilege or fair comment apply. The subsection thus reverses the rule, originally established in *Smith v. Streatfield* [1913] 3 K.B. 704 and applied in *Eglantine Inn Ltd v. Smith* [1948] N.I. 48, that, if malice is proved against the defendant who is the author of the statement, the defence of privilege is not available to any co-defendant (such as a printer) concerned in the publication. *Smith v. Streatfield*, however, was overruled by the English Court of Appeal in *Egger v. Viscount Chelmsford* [1965] 1 Q.B. 248 (on which see Newark (1965) 16 N.I.L.Q. 90) and does not appear to have been followed by Fitzgibbon J., in *Nevin v. Roddy* [1935] I.R. 397 at 423. The rule was also rejected by the Supreme Court of Canada in *Sun Life Assurance Co. of Canada v. Dalrymple* (1965) 50 D.L.R. (2d.) 217. McDonald, *op. cit.*, at 270, points out that where a number of persons are joint authors of a defamatory statement and they wish to rely on the defence of unintentional defamation, the subsection does not immunise one person against the malice of another because it omits to cover this particular defence.

Subsection (5), which replaces section 5 of the Law of Libel Amendment Act 1888, protects defendants against having to pay damages twice over for what is substantially the same damage. By enabling the court to find wrongdoers to be "concurrent wrongdoers", the subsection will allow contribution, whereas section 5 of the 1888 Act, though providing for apportionment, did not expressly allow for contribution. Moreover, section 5 was confined to libel and did not extent to slander or injurious falsehood.

Subsection (6) remedies an omission from the Statute of Limitations 1957 and provides that where a special period of limitation is prescribed for a particular tort, that period will also apply to an action for conspiracy to commit that tort. On the Statute of Limitations 1957 generally, see Brady and Kerr, *The Limitation of Actions in the Republic of Ireland* (2nd ed., 1994).

Extent of Liability

12.—(1) Subject to the provisions of sections 14, 38 and 46, concurrent wrongdoers are each liable for the whole of the damage in respect of which they are concurrent wrongdoers.

(2) Where the acts of two or more persons who are not concurrent wrong-

doers cause independent items of damage of the same kind to a third person or to one of their number, the court may apportion liability between such persons in such manner as may be justified by the probabilities of the case, or where the plaintiff is at fault may similarly reduce his damages; and if the proper proportions cannot be determined the damages may be apportioned or divided equally.

(3) Subsection (2) of this section shall apply to two or more persons whose acts taken together constitute a nuisance, even though the act of any one of them taken alone would not constitute a nuisance, not being unreasonable in degree.

GENERAL NOTE

This section deals with the extent of the liability of concurrent wrongdoers. The effect of subsection (1) is that all concurrent wrongdoers are liable *in solidum* for the whole of the damage subject to:

    (i)   the acceptance by the plaintiff of apportionment of his damages in accordance with section 14;

    (ii) contributory negligence on the part of the plaintiff;

    (iii) the special position of collisions at sea under section 46 (where the liability of two or more ships is determined by the degree of fault).

In other words, the plaintiff is entitled to recover a separate judgment for the whole amount of his damage against each concurrent wrongdoer (see also the annotation to section 14, page 17 *infra*).

The constitutionality of sections 12 and 14 was tested in *Iarnród Éireann v. Ireland* [1996] 3 I.R. 321, having regard to the provisions of Articles 40.3 and 43 of the Constitution. Irish Rail had been one of a number of defendants who had been sued following the derailment of a train after a collision with a herd of cattle. The trial judge, Johnson J., found that both Irish Rail and the cattle owner had been negligent and liability was apportioned at 30 per cent and 70 per cent respectively. As the cattle owner was a person "without any significant means", the consequence of sections 12 and 14 was that Irish Rail was obliged to compensate the injured passengers for all of the damage they had sustained in circumstances where it had been determined that its responsibility for the damage was only 30 per cent.

O'Flaherty J., delivering the unanimous judgment of the Supreme Court, said that there was nothing irrational or disproportionate about the two sections. The possibility that one of a number of defendants might be insolvent and unable to meet his or her liability was "an unfortunate aspect of litigation". If it transpired that Irish Rail would not be in a position to obtain any significant contribution from the cattle owner, that would not be because of any defect or injustice in the law, but simply because the cattle owner would not have had the assets to pay a significant contribution to Irish Rail. O'Flaherty J. felt that this was simply "one of the hard facts of life". Irish Rail, in his opinion, was in no worse a position than anyone else who had a claim against a wrongdoer who could not pay compensation because of a lack of means.

According to Keane J. in the High Court in *Iarnród Éireann v. Ireland* [1996] 3 I.R. 321 at 357, subsection (1), in providing that concurrent wrongdoers were to be each liable for the whole of the damage in respect of which they were concurrent wrongdoers, was declaratory of the common law.

Subsections (2) and (3) are declaratory of existing law in regard to two or more persons who were not "concurrent wrongdoers". Here there is no liability *in solidum*, but liability is apportioned according to the probabilities of the case and, if apportionment proves impossible, then liability will be divided equally.

Procedurally the matter is governed in the High Court by the Rules of the Superior Courts 1986 (S.I. No. 15 of 1986), Ord. 18, r. 1 and in the Circuit Court by Ord. 8, r. 1 of the Rules of the Circuit Court 1950 (S.I. No. 179 of 1950), both of which provide that a plaintiff may unite in the same action several causes of action but if it appears to the court that any such cause of action cannot be conveniently tried or disposed of together the court may order separate trials of any of such causes of action. Conversely, the Rules of the Superior Courts 1986, Ord. 49, r. 6 and Ord. 30, r. 6 of the Rules of the Circuit Court 1950 both provide that where a plaintiff has brought separate actions any party may apply to have them consolidated. As an alternative to consolidation the plaintiff or the defendant may seek to have the cases heard simultaneously. As to the court's discretion on such applications see *Malone v. Great Northern Railway Co.* [1931] I.R. 1; *O'Neill v. Ryanair Ltd (No. 2)* [1992] 1 I.R. 160; *Duffy v. Newsgroup Newspapers Ltd* [1992] I.L.R.M. 835 and *Murphy v. Times Newspapers Ltd*, unreported, Supreme Court, October 21, 1997. In *Duffy*, McCarthy J., speaking for the Supreme Court, set forth the applicable principles for a joint trial as follows:

(1) Is there a common question of law or fact of sufficient importance?
(2) Is there a substantial saving of expense or inconvenience?
(3) Is there a likelihood of confusion or miscarriage of justice?

In *Murphy*, O'Flaherty J., speaking for the Supreme Court, said that he took it to be agreed that, of the three, the necessity to make sure that a case was conducted in such a manner so that a just result could be achieved was the most important point and that the question of saving expense and convenience ranked last.

It should be noted that section 78 of the Courts of Justice Act 1936 provides that, where there are two or more defendants and the plaintiff succeeds against one or more of the defendants and fails against the others, or other of the defendants, it shall be lawful for the court, if having regard to all the circumstances it thinks proper so to do, to order that the defendant or defendants against whom the plaintiff has succeeded shall, in addition to the plaintiff's own costs, pay to the plaintiff by way of recoupment the costs which the plaintiff is liable to pay and pays to the defendant or defendants against whom he has failed. In deciding whether such an order should be made, the question which the court must answer is whether it was reasonable to join the successful defendants in the proceedings: see *Byrne v. Lancaster* [1958] Ir. Jur. Rep. 51 and *Clancy v. North End Garage (Wexford) Ltd* [1969] I.R. 122.

It has also been held that, by serving notice of discontinuance of an action against a defendant, a plaintiff can still bring himself or herself, within the terms of section 78. In *Wilson v. Minister for Finance* [1944] I.R. 142, where the first-named defendant had lodged money in court while denying liability, the plaintiff discontinued the action against the second-named defendant and applied for leave to accept the money lodged. The question arose whether the plaintiff was entitled to apply for an order under section 78 directing the first-named defendant to pay the costs which the plaintiff would otherwise have been liable to pay to the second-named defendant. The majority of the Supreme Court (Sullivan C.J., Murnaghan and Black JJ.) held that, by the acceptance of the money lodged in court and the service of the notice of discontinuance, the plaintiff had succeeded in the action against the first-named defendant and had failed in the action against the second-named defendant within the meaning of section 78. Accordingly, the first-named defendant had to pay to the plaintiff by way of recoupment the costs which the plaintiff was liable to pay to the second-named defendant.

The meaning of the phrase "in addition to the plaintiff's own costs" in section 78 was considered by the High Court in *Maher v. Great Northern Railway Co. (Ireland) (No. 2)* (1942) 76 I.L.T.R. 189. Maguire P. was of the view that "the language of the section seemed clear" and that the words of the section did not envisage the payment of the plaintiff's party- and party-costs against the successful defendant, but only the costs payable by the plaintiff to that defendant.

The provisions of subsection (2) were considered by the Supreme Court in *Byrne v. Triumph Engineering Ltd* [1982] I.R. 220. There, the plaintiff claimed damages for personal injuries sustained by him on two separate occasions. In June 1977, he suffered head injuries while working for the first-named defendant, who was a sub-contractor engaged by the second-named defendant. In October 1977, he suffered injuries to his wrist while working for the third-named defendant. The plaintiff issued a plenary summons against all three defendants. The defendants applied to the High Court, pursuant to what is now Rules of the Superior Courts 1986, Ord. 18, r. 1, for a ruling that it was not convenient for the claims to be tried together.

The application was refused by Hamilton J. (as he then was) and this decision was upheld by a majority of the Supreme Court. While the procedure adopted by the plaintiff in suing in the one action in respect of two distinct and separate causes of action involving the joinder of unrelated defendants was regarded as unusual, nevertheless it was permitted by the Rules of the Superior Courts, subject to the rights of any of the defendants to apply for separate trials. O'Higgins C.J. was of the view that section 12(2) covered the kind of situation which arose in these proceedings. However, he added:

> The subsection deals only with the Court's power to apportion at the trial. In my view, it does not affect the procedure laid down in the Rules of the Superior Courts as to the circumstances in which such a joinder of causes of action against different defendants may be brought to trial.

Kenny J., in his dissenting judgment, noted that section 12(2) recognised that a joint action may be brought but that it did not affect the right of the defendants to apply for a separate trial. He continued:

> Section 12(2) of the Act of 1961 allows a plaintiff who has the misfortune to be involved in two wholly unconnected accidents to sue the two defendants who, he says, were responsible for the accidents. It does not determine whether it is convenient to try the two causes of action together. Despite subsection (2) of section 12 the Court may order separate trials of the two causes of action.

Joinder of defendants

13.—An action may be brought against all of concurrent wrongdoers or against any of them without joining the other or others, but the court shall have power—

    (a) in an action for the execution of trusts, to require the trust estate to be properly represented;

    (b) in an action where the title to property is in question, to require the joinder of all those interested or claiming to be interested in the property.

GENERAL NOTE

This section, which permits an action to be brought against all of the concurrent wrong-doers, or against any of them without joining the other or others is, according to the Explanatory Memorandum accompanying the Bill, largely declaratory of the existing law for tortfeasors but is largely legislative for contractors and trustees. It should be noted that, although the plaintiff need not join all the concurrent wrongdoers, any wrongdoer sued may claim contribution from a fellow concurrent wrongdoer by serving a third-party notice under section 27(1).

Judgments to be several

14.—(1) Where judgment is given against concurrent wrongdoers who are sued together, the court may give judgment against the defendants together or against the defendants separately and, if the judgment is given against the defendants together, it shall take effect as if it were given against them separately.

(2) Subject to subsections (3) and (6) of this section and to sections 38 and 46, each of the said judgments shall be for the full amount of the plaintiff's

damages in respect of which the defendants are concurrent wrongdoers, together with any further damages in respect of which the particular defendant against whom judgment is given is individually liable and, if the same jury has in its verdict apportioned damages between the defendants on the basis that the total of the damages awarded is meant to be equivalent to the plaintiff's loss resulting from the concurrent wrongs, the plaintiff shall be entitled to judgment against the defendants for the aggregate of such damages.

(3) The plaintiff may agree to accept an apportionment of his damages among the defendants according to their degrees of fault and, in this event, the following provisions shall take effect—

    (a) satisfaction of one judgment shall not operate as satisfaction of the others;

    (b) the defendants shall have no right of contribution among themselves;

    (c) the plaintiff, at any time within the period limited by law for the enforcement of judgments and upon proof that, after taking reasonable steps, he has failed to obtain satisfaction of any judgment in whole or in part, shall have liberty to apply for secondary judgments having the effect of distributing the deficiency among the other defendants in such proportions as may be just and equitable.

(4) Where the court would be prepared to award punitive damages against one of concurrent tortfeasors, punitive damages shall not be awarded against another of such tortfeasors merely because he is a concurrent tortfeasor, but a judgment for an additional sum by way of punitive damages may be given against the first-mentioned tortfeasor.

(5) The judgment mentioned in subsection (4) of this section may specify that such additional sum is awarded by way of punitive damages, and no contribution shall be payable in respect thereof by a tortfeasor against whom such judgment could not properly have been given.

(6) Where, in an action for libel or slander, one of concurrent tortfeasors would have been entitled to a mitigation of the damages payable by him had he been a single tortfeasor, but another of the said tortfeasors would not have been so entitled, the first-mentioned tortfeasor shall be entitled to the said mitigation of damages and shall not be compellable to make contribution except in respect of the amount of damages payable by him; and the judgment against him may be given accordingly.

GENERAL NOTE

This section abolishes the common law rule that where joint tortfeasors were sued together no more than a single judgment could be rendered against those who were held liable: see *Heydon's Case* (1612) 11 Co. Rep. 5a, applied in *Dawson v. M'Clelland* [1899] 2 I.R. 486 and *Johnson v. Larkin* [1926] 2 I.R. 40.

Subsection (1) provides that, where judgment is given against concurrent wrongdoers, judgment may be given against them separately or together and that judgment given against them separately or together will take effect as if it were given against them separately.

Subsection (2) provides that each of the judgments is to be for the full amount of the plaintiff's damages and, if the damages are apportioned on the basis that the total of the apportionments is to be equivalent to the plaintiff's loss, the plaintiff will be entitled to judgment against the defendants for the aggregate of the damages. This is, however, subject to subsections (3) and (6) and to section 38 (liability of concurrent wrongdoers where the plaintiff is guilty of contributory negligence) and section 46 (collisions at sea).

Subsection (3) allows a plaintiff to accept an apportionment of his damages and, in such a case, the defendants will have no right to contribution. Although subsection (4) refers to "punitive damages" the Supreme Court has held, in *Conway v. Irish National Teachers' Organisation* [1991] 2 I.R. 305, that punitive and exemplary damages must be recognised as constituting the same element. All three members of the Court (Finlay C.J., Griffin and McCarthy JJ..) preferred to refer to this type of damages as "exemplary damages". The subsection represents an exception to the general rule regarding "concurrent wrongdoers" but it is unclear, given that the subsection uses the undefined phrase "concurrent tortfeasors", whether it is relevant to circumstances where the liability of the concurrent tortfeasors is vicarious: see McCarthy J. in *McIntyre v. Lewis* [1991] 1 I.R. 121 at 139. As the Law Reform Commission point out in their *Consultation Paper on Aggravated, Exemplary and Restitutionary Damages* (April 1998) at paragraph 7.53, if vicariously liable individuals were included within the meaning of concurrent tortfeasors, then exemplary damages could not be awarded against vicariously liable employers unless they were liable to exemplary damages in their own right. Subsection (6) deals with the case where one of concurrent tortfeasors in a defamation action would have been entitled to a mitigation of the damages had he been a single tortfeasor.

Judgment by default

15.—(1) Where one of concurrent wrongdoers who are sued together makes default of appearance or defence, the plaintiff may obtain an interlocutory judgment against him and damages shall be assessed against him-

    (a) at the same time as damages are assessed at the trial against the other defendants who appear;

    (b) if the plaintiff fails against such other defendants or discontinues his action against them, separately under the interlocutory judgment.

(2) If the plaintiff fails against the defendants who appear for a reason that goes to the liability of all, the interlocutory judgment shall be discharged.

(3) If the plaintiff's damages against the defendants who appear are reduced under subsection (1) of section 34 on account of the plaintiff's contributory negligence, damages shall be assessed under the interlocutory judgment as if the defendant had appeared.

(4) This section shall not apply to any head of damage in respect of which the defendant who makes default and the defendants who appear are not concurrent wrongdoers.

GENERAL NOTE

For judgment in default of appearance see the Rules of the Superior Courts 1986, Ord. 13; for judgment in default of defence see the Rules of the Superior Courts 1986, Ord. 27, rr. 8 and 9.

Note that the Rules of the Superior Courts 1986, Ord. 27, r. 10 provide that:

> Where, in any action as mentioned in rule 8, there are several defendants, then, if one of such defendants make such default as aforesaid, the plaintiff may either (if the cause of action is severable) set down the action at once on motion for judgment against the defendant so making default, or may set it down against him at the time when it is entered for trial or set down on motion for judgment against the other defendants.

Discharge and estoppel by satisfaction

16.—(1) Where damage is suffered by any person as a result of concurrent wrongs, satisfaction by any wrongdoer shall discharge the others whether such others have been sued to judgment or not.

(2) Satisfaction means payment of damages, whether after judgment or by way of accord and satisfaction, or the rendering of any agreed substitution therefor.

(3) If the payment is of damages, it must be of the full damages agreed by the injured person or adjudged by the court as the damages due to him in respect of the wrong; otherwise it shall operate only as partial satisfaction.

(4) An injured person who has accepted satisfaction from one alleged to be a wrongdoer, whether under a judgment or otherwise, shall, in any subsequent proceeding against another wrongdoer in respect of the same damage, be estopped from denying that the person who made the satisfaction was liable to him; and the liability of such person shall be conclusively assumed for the purpose of the said proceeding; but the injured person may litigate in the said proceeding any question of law or fact relative to the liability of the defendant to such proceeding, other than the question whether or not the said satisfaction was made by one liable to the injured person.

GENERAL NOTE

Subsections (1), (2) and (3) are "probably" declaratory of the common law, *per* McCarthy J., *Murphy v. J. Donohoe Ltd* [1992] I.L.R.M. 378 at 394 and subsection (4) deals with the case of satisfaction by a person who is subsequently found not to be a wrongdoer at all and therefore a stranger. The injured person is estopped from denying that the stranger was liable thus preventing the possibility of double satisfaction. See also section 29(1) (page 35 *infra*).

In *Murphy*, a majority of the Supreme Court (McCarthy, O'Flaherty and Egan JJ., Finlay C.J. and Hederman J., dissenting) held that a settlement of the claim as between one defendant and the infant plaintiffs on terms that money would be paid into Court and that proceedings would issue against all the defendants did not amount to an "accord and satisfaction". For the position in England see the decision of the House of Lords in *Jameson v. Central Electricity Generating Board* [1999] 2 W.L.R. 141.

Release of, or accord with, one wrongdoer

17.—(1) The release of or accord with, one concurrent wrongdoer shall discharge the others if such release or accord indicates an intention that the others are to be discharged.

(2) If no such intention is indicated by such release or accord, the other wrongdoers shall not be discharged but the injured person shall be identified with the person with whom the release or accord is made in any action against the other wrongdoers in accordance with paragraph (h) of subsection (1) of section 35, and in any such action the claim against the other wrongdoers shall be reduced in the amount of the consideration paid for the release or accord, or in any amount by which the release or accord provides that the total claim shall be reduced, or to the extent that the wrongdoer with whom the release or accord was made would have been liable to contribute if the plaintiff's total claim had been paid by the other wrongdoers, whichever of those three amounts is the greatest.

(3) For the purpose of his Part, the taking of money out of court that has been paid in by a defendant shall be deemed to be an accord and satisfaction with him.

Subsection (1) is in large part declaratory, except that it extends to several concurrent tortfeasors who possibly would not have been discharged by a release or accord with one of their number even though such release or accord expressly so provided.

Subsection (2) sweeps away the subtle distinctions between a release and a covenant not to sue and clarifies the law relating to accord and satisfaction. Prior to the Act the release of one of several joint tortfeasors released all the others (see *Duck v. Mayeu* [1892] 2 Q.B. 511 at 513), even though this was not in the contemplation of the parties, but an agreement on the part of the plaintiff not to sue one of the defendants did not prejudice his right to proceed against the others. This was because the release was seen as extinguishing the cause of action: *Cuttler v. McPhail* [1962] Q.B. 292 at 296. According to Glanville Williams, *JTCN*, p. 504, the subsection is based on the desirability of facilitating out of court settlements and the principle that partial satisfaction by one concurrent wrongdoer operates in favour of all. To prevent collusion between the injured person and one wrongdoer whereby the injured person obtained in aggregate more than the amount of the damages to which he was justly entitled, Glanville Williams, *ibid.*, recommended the use of the words "in the amount of the consideration paid for the release or accord". This has the consequence that the claim against the other wrongdoers is reduced even though the release or accord stipulates that the money paid shall be regarded as consideration for the release or accord and not as satisfaction of the liability. Although the word "accord" (unlike the word "satisfaction") is not defined by the Act it means "an agreement that is a release in all respects except that it is not under seal": *per* Egan J. in *Murphy v. J. Donohoe Ltd* [1992] I.L.R.M. 378 at 396.

Subsection (3) altered the pre-existing law as to the taking out of money paid into court by one wrongdoer by providing that, if the plaintiff takes money out of court paid in by one concurrent wrongdoer, he will be barred against that wrongdoer but not against any other except to the extent stated in subsection (2).

Judgment against one wrongdoer

18.—(1) Where damage is suffered by any person as a result of concurrent wrongs—

    (a) Judgment recovered against any wrongdoer liable in respect of that damage shall not be a bar to an action against any other person who would, if sued, have been liable as concurrent wrongdoer in respect of the same damage;

    (b) if more than one action is brought in respect of that damage by or on behalf of the person by whom it was suffered, or for the benefit of his estate, or for the benefit of his dependants, against wrongdoers liable in respect of the damage, the sums recoverable under the judgments given in those actions by way of damages shall not in the aggregate exceed the amount of the damages awarded by the judgment first given; and in any of those actions, other than that in which judgment is first given, the plaintiff shall not be entitled to costs unless the court is of opinion that there was reasonable ground for bringing the action: but this paragraph shall not apply where the judgment first given was an apportioned judgment given in pursuance of section 14, section 38 or section 46.

(2) The reference in this section to "the judgment first given" shall, in a

case where that judgment is reversed on appeal, be construed as a reference to the judgment first given which is not so reversed and, in a case where a judgment is varied on appeal, be construed as a reference to that judgment as so varied.

GENERAL NOTE

Before the enactment of the Tortfeasors Act 1951, judgment against one joint tortfeasor discharged the others in respect of that tort, even though it produced no fruits, whereas judgment against one of several concurrent tortfeasors did not bar an action against another, and in the second action, the plaintiff might obtain a larger judgment than in the first. The 1951 Act rectified this anomaly by providing that judgment against one tortfeasor was not a bar to an action against another tortfeasor (section 2) and that the plaintiff was not entitled to recover more in the second action than the amount awarded in the first (section 3). The object of these two sections was to prevent injustice to a plaintiff who found that the tortfeasor he had chosen to sue was insolvent and not to allow a plaintiff who was dissatisfied with the assessment of damages in the first action to sue another in the hope of obtaining a more favourable assessment. Section 18 follows the principle of sections 2 and 3 of the 1951 Act, but applies it to all concurrent wrongdoers.

The provisions of subsection (1)(b) were considered by Costello P. in *McSorley v. O'Mahony*, unreported, High Court, November 6, 1996, who pointed out that the subsection was in terms similar to section 6(1)(b) of the English Law Reform (Married Women and Tortfeasors) Act 1935 in respect of which Glanville Williams had commented in *JTCN*, p. 39, that the object of the 1935 Act was "to prevent injustice to a plaintiff who finds that the tortfeasor whom he has chosen to sue is insolvent". It was no part of the Act's policy "that a plaintiff who has sued one tortfeasor, and who is dissatisfied with the assessment of his damages by the court, should be allowed to sue the other tortfeasor in the hope of obtaining a greater bite from the cherry". Accordingly, section 6(1)(b) of the English Act of 1935 expressly provided that a plaintiff could not recover more than the sum awarded by the judgment in the first action.

Judgment in favour of one alleged wrongdoer

19.—(1) Where the injured person sues one or more of alleged concurrent wrongdoers and judgment is given for one defendant, the injured person shall be bound by the findings of fact in favour of such defendant in the injured person's present or subsequent action against another or others of the alleged concurrent wrongdoers.

    (2) (a) For the purpose of subsection (1) of this section, where judgment is given for the said defendant on the ground of the injured person's discontinuance, the injured person shall be bound by the allegations and denials in the said defendant's defence as if they had been found in favour of the said defendant, so far as they are relevant to the defence of that defendant.

        (b) Paragraph (a) of this subsection shall not apply unless, on the facts, the injured person is barred by his discontinuance from bringing a second action against the said defendant.

    (3) Where an action is brought against concurrent wrongdoers and judgment is given against one and for another for a reason that goes to the liability of all, the first-mentioned judgment shall be discharged.

    (4) Where an action is brought against concurrent wrongdoers and judgment is given against one without reduction of damages and against another subject to a reduction of damages under subsection (1) of section 34 on account of the

plaintiff's contributory negligence, the damages under the first-mentioned judgment shall be assessed subject to the same proportionate reduction, and the provisions of section 38 shall apply.

GENERAL NOTE

For discontinuance, see the Rules of the Superior Courts 1986, Ord. 26, r. 1, which allows a plaintiff to discontinue the action against all or any of the defendants, on payment of such defendant's taxed costs, and provides that such a discontinuance shall not be a defence to any subsequent action. Ord. 26, r. 4, however, provides that, if any subsequent action shall be brought before payment of the costs of a discontinued action, for the same, or substantially the same, cause of action, the court may order a stay of such subsequent action, until such costs shall have been paid.

Limitation of actions against one of concurrent wrongdoers

20.—For the purpose of the Statute of Limitations or any other limitation enactment concealed fraud by one of concurrent wrongdoers shall not suspend time for another or others.

GENERAL NOTE

This section provides that concealed fraud by one concurrent wrongdoer will not suspend time for another or others for the purposes of the Statutes of Limitations 1957 and 1991, or any other limitation enactment. On "concealed fraud" see Brady and Kerr, *op. cit.*, pp. 188–196.

CHAPTER II

Contribution between Concurrent Wrongdoers

Contribution in respect of damages

21.—(1) Subject to the provisions of this Part, a concurrent wrongdoer (for this purpose called the claimant) may recover contribution from any other wrongdoer who is, or would if sued at the time of the wrong have been, liable in respect of the same damage (for this purpose called the contributor), so, however, that no person shall be entitled to recover contribution under this Part from any person entitled to be indemnified by him respect of the liability in respect of which the contribution is sought.

(2) In any proceedings for contribution under this Part, the amount of the contribution recoverable from any contributor shall be such as may be found by the court to be just and equitable having regard to the degree of that contributor's fault, and the court shall have power to exempt any person from liability to make contribution or to direct that the contribution to be recovered from any contributor shall amount to a complete indemnity.

GENERAL NOTE

This section provides for contribution between concurrent wrongdoers in respect of damages and follows the principle of section 5 of the Tortfeasors Act 1951. Section 5 had abrogated the common law rule that there was no contribution between joint tortfeasors. This remarkably harsh rule had been established by the decision in *Merryweather v. Nixan* (1799) 8 T.R. 186 and was to the effect that, where a plaintiff recovered the full amount of his judgment from one out of two or more joint tortfeasors, the tortfeasor who had satisfied the judgment could not recover contribution from any of the other tortfeasors by reason of the operation of the maxim *ex turpi causa non oritur actio*. The rule was extended in *Horwell v. London Omnibus Co.* (1877) 2 Ex. D. 365 to concurrent tortfeasors whose independent actions caused the same damage.

Subsection (1) applies to all wrongdoers, whereas the 1951 Act applied only to tortfeasors. But a claim against a third-party for a contribution or indemnity will only succeed if it can be shown that the third-party committed a "wrong" in respect of which the injured plaintiff could have sued the third-party (*per* Costello J. in *Staunton v. Toyota (Ireland) Ltd*, unreported, High Court, April 15, 1988). This proposition is well illustrated by the decision of the Supreme Court in *Conole v. Redbank Oyster Co.* [1976] I.R. 191. The defendant's motor vessel capsized, drowning a number of passengers. The vessel had been built by F Ltd and was unseaworthy when delivered to the defendants. The personal representative of one of the drowned passengers, claimed damages against the owners of the vessel and they claimed contribution from F Ltd. The claim failed because, even assuming that F Ltd had been negligent, the plaintiff on the facts of the case could not have sued F Ltd as their default had not been, the *causa causans* of the accident. Because F Ltd did not rank as a concurrent wrongdoer, no claim for a contribution or indemnity arose.

Payment on foot of a judgment for damages is not necessary to establish the right to contribution. Subsection (1) provides that a concurrent wrongdoer may recover contribution from any other wrongdoer "who is, or would if sued at the time of the wrong have been, liable in respect of the same damage". The ordinary meaning of the word "liable" is that a person is under an obligation enforceable by legal process (see *George Wimpey & Co. Ltd v. British Overseas Airways Corporation* [1955] A.C. 169 and *Bitumen & Oil Refineries (Australia) Ltd v. Commissioner for Government Transport* (1955) 92 C.L.R. 200). For the purposes of the 1961 Act, however, "liable" is defined as referring to legal liability whether enforceable by action or not. In typical cases of injury caused by two wrongdoers, both will be "liable" to the victim in the ordinary sense of the word. In certain cases, however, one wrongdoer will not be liable because of some immunity or other defence. An example given in the Explanatory Memorandum accompanying the Bill was the liability as a concurrent wrongdoer of a person who damages the property of a deceased person before the executor obtains probate. Another example would be the immunity provided in section 12 of the Industrial Relations Act 1990 to a member or official of an authorised trade union, *i.e.* a trade union with a negotiation licence who, in contemplation or furtherance of a trade dispute, has induced the breach of a contract of employment.

Glanville Williams argued that persons under an unenforceable liability should still be considered liable for the purposes of tortfeasor statutes (*JTCN*, pp. 99–110). Such an unenforceable liability would exist when there was a "defence which is a complete defence to the action . . . and yet . . . is not sufficient to take away all wrongful quality from the act". It is essential, therefore, to distinguish between cases, where there is an unenforceable liability, such as where injury is caused by the carelessness of someone who owes the victim a duty of care but at the same time enjoys diplomatic immunity, and cases where there is no liability at all, such as where injury is caused by the carelessness of someone who does not owe the victim a duty of care. In the latter situation, it is not the case of a special defence preventing the victim from obtaining judgment, but of one of the essential elements of liability being absent. Kutner in (1985) 63 Can. Bar Rev. 1 at 7 doubts whether this is a workable distinction outside those cases where the special defence is the Statute of Frauds or the Statute of Limitations. If a victim cannot recover damages, he asks, because before the act complained of, he agreed to waive his legal rights in respect of it (see annotation to section 34, page 40 *infra*) or because the court applies the *ex turpi causa* maxim (see annotation to section 57, page 67 *infra*) is this because of a defence to liability for wrongful conduct or because one of the essential elements of liability is absent?

The meaning of the words "who is, or would if sued . . . have been, liable in respect of the same damage" contained in the equivalent New South Wales legislation (Law Reform (Miscellaneous Provisions) Act 1946, section 5) was considered by the High Court of Australia in *James Hardie & Coy Pty Ltd v. Seltsam Pty Ltd* (1998) 73 A.L.J.R. 238. The facts were as follows: P sued three defendants D1, D2 and D3 as concurrent tortfeasors. D1 claimed against D3 seeking indemnity and contribution. D3 cross claimed for corresponding relief against D1 and D2. P, D1 and D2 reached a settlement and judgment was entered for P in the agreed amounts against D1 and D2. P and D3 then settled on terms adverse to P and judgment was entered in favour of D3. D3 then applied to have the claim by DI for contribution struck out. The High Court of Australia, by a majority, held that D1's claim should be struck out. The judgment which, albeit by consent, determined conclusively as between P and D3 that D3 was not liable put an end to D1's claim for contribution because D3 was no longer within the class of persons against whom an order for contribution could be made. The Court rejected DI's submission that D3 had not been "sued to judgment" in the sense required to deny D3 the character of a person "not yet sued". D3 had been sued and the second limb of the provision was thus inapplicable as being confined in its terms to a case where the respondent to the claim for contribution had not been sued but would, if sued, have been held liable. As various members of the majority observed, the problem was largely of D1's own making. At the very least D1 could have sought deferral of the entry of judgment in favour of D3 until the issue of D3's liability to P for the purposes of D1's contribution claim had been determined.

The amount of the contribution recoverable is such as is just and equitable having regard to the degree of the contributor's fault. In *Patterson v. Murphy* [1978] I.L.R.M. 85, Costello J. held at 101, that this provision should be interpreted in the same way as the Supreme Court in *Carroll v. Clare County Council* [1975] I.R. 221, had interpreted the similar provision in section 34. He therefore considered the blameworthiness of the contribution which each defendant made to the damages which the plaintiffs suffered by reason of the acts complained of "the test of blameworthiness being an objective one and applied by reference to what a reasonable man of woman would have done in the circumstances of the present case." See also Costello J. in *Ward v. McMaster* [1985] I.R. 29 at 54–55 and Blayney J. in *Connolly v. Dundalk U.D.C.*, unreported, Supreme Court, November 18, 1992.

The court is empowered by this section to direct that the contribution should amount to a complete indemnity: see *Staunton v. Toyota (Ireland) Ltd*, unreported, High Court, April 15, 1988. Note that the Rules of the Superior Courts 1986, Ord. 16, r.12, provide that one defendant may make a claim for indemnity or contribution against another defendant without the leave of the Court by issuing and serving a notice making such claim. No appearance to such a notice is necessary.

Contribution claimed by settling tortfeasor

22.—(1) Where the claimant has settled with the injured person in such a way as to bar the injured person's claim against the other concurrent wrongdoers, the claimant may recover contribution in the same way as if he had suffered judgment for damages, if he satisfies the court that the amount of the settlement was reasonable; and if the court finds that the amount of the settlement was excessive, it may fix the amount at which the claim should have been settled.

(2) Where the claimant has settled with the injured person without barring the injured person's claim against the other concurrent wrongdoers or has paid to the injured person a sum on account of his damages, the claimant shall have the same right of contribution as aforesaid, and for this purpose the payment of a reasonable consideration for a release or accord shall be regarded as a payment of damages for which the claimant is liable to the injured person: but the contributor shall have the right to claim repayment of the whole or part of the sum so paid if the said contributor is subsequently compelled to pay a sum in settlement of his own liability to the injured person and if the circumstances render repayment just and equitable.

This section is concerned with contributions claimed by a settling wrongdoer. According to the Explanatory Memorandum accompanying the Bill, the object of this section was to encourage settlements out of court. Subsection (1), which deals with the case of a claimant who settles with the injured person in such a way as to bar the injured person's claim against the other wrongdoers, is based on section 1 of the Ontario Negligence Act 1948. Subsection (2), which is in similar terms to section 3 of the Ontario Negligence Act 1970, covers the case where the settlement does not bar the injured person's claim against the other wrongdoer and provides that the claimant will have the same right of contribution as under subsection (1). The subsection also provides that the contributor may recover from the claimant the whole or part of the sum paid as contribution. For example, the injured person (P) settles with a wrongdoer (D1, the claimant) for £6,000 and D1 obtains £3,000 from another wrongdoer (D2, the contributor) in a claim for contribution, both being held equally to blame. In a subsequent action by P against D2, if P recovers £4,000 out of a total assessed damages of £10,000, D2 would pay in all £7,000 but D2 will be entitled to recover from D1 the whole or part of the contribution he has already paid. Consequently, he should recover £2,000, which makes his final liability £5,000 and D1's final liability will also be £5,000.

Enforcement of judgment for contribution

23.—(1) Where, in accordance with the provisions of this Part, judgment is given for contribution in respect of damages for which the claimant is or has been liable to the injured person, execution shall not be issued on such judgment until after satisfaction by the claimant in whose favour it is given before or after the said judgment of the whole or part of the damages for which he is liable to the injured person, and execution shall then issue only in respect of the amount by which the sum paid by him exceeds his just proportion of that particular amount, as such proportion is determined by the court in accordance with this Part.

(2) Notwithstanding anything in subsection (1) of this section, execution may be issued on such judgment as aforesaid after satisfaction by the claimant in whose favour it is given of his just proportion of the damages for which he is liable to the injured person, provided that in this case the court makes provision, by obtaining the personal undertaking of the claimant's solicitor or otherwise, for applying the sum received under the said judgment towards satisfaction of the damages due to the injured person.

(3) In this section "damages for which he is liable to the injured person" means damages for which the claimant is liable at the time when satisfaction is made to the injured person or his representatives or lawful assignees.

(4) A payment of damages by the claimant at a time when the injured person's cause of action against the claimant is barred by the Statute of Limitations or any other limitation enactment shall not found a claim to levy execution under a judgment for contribution: but such a payment shall found such a claim if, at the time when it was made, the injured person's cause of action against the contributor was not barred.

This section provides for the enforcement of a judgment for contribution. Subsection (1) distinguishes between the right to obtain a judgment for contribution and the right to levy execution under that judgment. According to the Explanatory Memorandum accompanying the Bill, it was convenient, where the injured person brings an action, that the issue of contribution should be disposed of in that action even though, since the plaintiff's claim has not been satisfied, an executable judgment for contribution cannot yet be obtained.

Subsection (2) allows execution of a judgment for contribution where the claimant has satisfied only his own just proportion of the damages, provided the claimant undertakes to apply the sum received under the judgment towards satisfaction of the injured person's damages.

Subsection (4) deals with the situation caused by the Statutes of Limitations 1957 and 1991 barring only the remedy not the right. Consequently, the claimant for contribution is liable to the injured person even after the period of limitation has expired. The subsection, however, provides that payment of damages in respect of a statute-barred liability will not give a right to contribution, except where the Statutes operate unevenly between the wrong-doers.

Contribution in respect of costs

24.—A judgment for contribution may be given in respect of costs payable to the injured person or incurred by the claimant but, where the injured person has sued the claimant and the contributor together and has recovered judgment for costs against both of them, the provisions of section 23 shall apply, with the substitution of the word "costs" for the word "damages" wherever it there appears.

GENERAL NOTE

Section 5 of the Tortfeasors Act 1951, being general in its wording, was not considered as allowing for contribution in respect of costs. This section, however, clearly allows for contribution in respect of costs payable to the injured person or incurred by the claimant. Where the claimant and the contributor are sued together, judgment for contribution in respect of costs will be subject to the same safeguards as judgment for contribution in respect of damages under section 23. The judgment is thus contingent upon the claimant satisfying the whole or part of the injured person's costs, or upon an undertaking by the claimant's solicitor to apply any sum received under the judgment in satisfaction of the cost due to the injured person.

The basis on which contribution to costs should be determined was considered by the Supreme Court in *Gillespie v. Fitzpatrick* [1970] I.R. 102. In their view, what is now the Rules of the Superior Courts 1986, Ord. 99, r. 1(1) provided that the matter of contribution was left to the trial judge's discretion to make such order as he or she might think proper:

> Therefore, a trial judge in an action such as this must consider in a judicial fashion what is fair and proper to do in the circumstances.

Here the trial judge, in determining the ratio of the contributions towards costs as between the two defendants, followed closely the proportions of the percentages of fault of the defendants. The Supreme Court refused to disturb the order as to costs since the Court felt that he had adopted "a very fair and reasonable method of dealing with the matter of contribution". Budd J., however, did add that, if it could be shown that one of the defendants was, by the nature of his pleadings and conduct of the action or the nature of his defence, responsible for the greater part of the costs of the action, then it might well be right and proper to visit that defendant with a higher proportion of the costs than that which he or she would have to bear on an apportionment of costs in accordance with his or her proportion of the degrees of fault.

One wrongdoer omitted from claim for contribution; contribution in respect of contribution

25.—Where, of three or more concurrent wrongdoers, one is omitted from the claim for contribution, contribution shall be awarded to the claimant on the basis that responsibility for the damage is to be borne by the claimant and the contributor or contributors without regard to the responsibility of the omitted wrongdoer, and, in such a case, a claimant whose net remaining liability is increased or a contributor whose contribution is increased by reason of the fact that judgment has not been given against the omitted wrongdoer may claim contribution from such admitted wrongdoer in accordance with the provisions of this Part: but, where such last-mentioned claim for contribution is made by a contributor in respect of his own liability to make contribution and judgment is given in such contributor's favour, execution shall not be issued on that judgment—

    (a) except in accordance with the provisions of section 23, with the substitution of "contribution" for "damages" and of "original claimant for contribution" for "injured person" wherever they there appear, and "just proportion" in the said section being understood to mean for this purpose just proportion as between the contributor in whose favour judgment for contribution is now given and the wrongdoer against whom the said judgment is given, and in any case

    (b) to an amount greater than the sum that, when added to the amount (if any) still due to the injured person, will equal the just proportion of the damages payable by the wrongdoer against whom the said judgment is given.

GENERAL NOTE

This section provides for the case where one wrongdoer is omitted from the claim for contribution. Here contribution is to be awarded to the claimant on the basis that responsibility for the damage is to be borne by the claimant and the contributors without regard to the responsibility of the omitted wrongdoer. Take the example of three concurrent wrongdoers (D1, D2 and D3) equally responsible to the injured person (P). P. sues D1, who joins only D2 in a claim for contribution, and the total damages are assessed at £9,000. The sum awarded to D1 by way of contribution will be £4,500. D1 may then claim contribution in respect of £1,500 (one-sixth of the total) from D3, if D1 can satisfy the Court (in accordance with section 27) that it was not reasonably practicable to join D3 in the original proceedings by P. D2 may do likewise.

D1's judgment against D3, however, will only be executable on the same conditions (see section 23) as his judgment against D2. D2 must also satisfy conditions similar to those imposed on D1. D2 must have paid D1 the whole or part of the contribution due or have paid to D1 the whole of D2's just proportion (*i.e.* one-third) of the damages and satisfy the Court that the sum recovered from D3 will be paid to D1. D2, however, cannot have an executable judgment against D3 unless D3 is safe from a further claim by P. in respect of the sum paid by D3 to D2. D2, therefore, cannot levy execution against D3 to an amount greater than the sum that, when added to the amount still due to P, will equal D3's just proportion (one-third) of the damages, that is, £3,000.

Contribution where property is restored to its owner

26.—For the purpose of a claim for contribution—

    (a) a person who restores property to its true owner shall be deemed to be a concurrent wrongdoer with one through whom he originally claimed the property and who was a wrongdoer in respect of it towards the true owner, and

(b) such restoration of property shall, as against such wrongdoer, be deemed to be a payment of damages to the extent of the value of the property.

GENERAL NOTE

This section provides for contribution or indemnity where property is restored. So if D1 converts P's property and as a result the property comes into the hands of D2, who restores it to P, D2 will have a claim for contribution against D1 to the same extent as if he had paid damages for conversion, regardless of whether D2 committed conversion or not.

Procedure for claiming contribution

27.—(1) A concurrent wrongdoer who is sued for damages or for contribution and who wishes to make a claim for contribution under this Part—

(a) shall not, if the person from whom he proposes to claim contribution is already a party to the action, be entitled to claim contribution except by a claim made in the said action, whether before or after judgment in the action; and

(b) shall, if the said person is not already a party to the action, serve a third-party notice upon such person as soon as is reasonably possible and, having served such notice, he shall not be entitled to claim contribution except under the third-party procedure. If such third-party notice is not served as aforesaid, the court may in its discretion refuse to make an order for contribution against the person from whom contribution is claimed.

(2) The provisions of subsection (1) of this section shall not apply to any contribution claim where the parties to the claim are precluded by agreement or otherwise from disputing any earlier determination by a court of the amount of the injured person's damages and the proportion in which contribution should be made.

(3) Where it is sought to serve a third-party notice making a claim for contribution, or making a claim for damages in respect of a wrong committed to the third-party plaintiff such claim for damages having arisen in whole or in part out of the same facts as the facts giving rise to the principal plaintiff's claim, leave to serve a third-party notice shall not be refused merely because the issue between the third-party plaintiff and the third-party will involve a difficult question of law.

(4) Where a concurrent wrongdoer makes a payment to the injured person without action in settlement of the injured person's claim against himself and subsequently claims contribution in accordance with section 22, the contributor shall have the right to have the injured person joined as co-defendant for the purpose of binding him by the determination of the proportions of contribution, unless the injured person is co-plaintiff in the action or the injured person has effectively agreed to be bound by such determination or the injured person has no claim against the contributor or the injured person has already sued the contributor to judgment.

[(5) A claim may be made or a notice may be served pursuant to subsection (1) of this section notwithstanding that the person making the claim or serving the notice denies or does not admit that he is a wrongdoer, and the making of the claim or serving of the notice shall not be taken as implying any admission of liability by him.]

GENERAL NOTE

This section deals with the procedure for claiming contribution. Its object is to ensure that, where practicable, claims for contribution will be made and determined in the injured person's action.

Subsection (1) was considered by the Supreme Court in *Cullen v. Clein* [1970] I.R. 146. The plaintiffs and the defendant were involved in a car accident and the defendant, who was denying negligence and loss, also made a counterclaim seeking a contribution from the first plaintiff in respect of the second plaintiff's claim. On the trial of the counterclaim, O'Keeffe P. apportioned one-third of the fault for the second plaintiff's injuries to the first plaintiff and ordered the latter to pay to the defendant a sum equal to one-third of the damages recovered by the second plaintiff. The first plaintiff appealed to the Supreme Court disputing, *inter alia* the maintainability of a claim for contribution made by way of counterclaim.

Ó Dálaigh C.J., with whom Walsh and McLoughlin JJ. agreed, examined Part III of the Act and section 27(1) in particular, and concluded that it was clear that not only were the proceedings brought by the defendant maintainable, but that unless he had made his claim by way of counterclaim in the action he would have found himself precluded from addressing any such claim. The Chief Justice continued:

> The defendant was a wrongdoer who was sued for damages by Mrs Cullen and he claimed to be a concurrent wrongdoer with Dr Cullen against whom he claimed contribution in respect of the damages suffered by Mrs Cullen. Dr Cullen was already a party to Mrs Cullen's action as a co-plaintiff, his claim being in respect of the damage to his car and out-of-pocket expenses. Service of a third-party notice under paragraph (b) was therefore inappropriate; but, while it may be that paragraph (a) had chiefly in contemplation the case in which the contributor was a co-defendant of the claimant, as the paragraph, in terms, speaks of a party to the action, it covers the case where the contributor is a plaintiff in the action as well as the commoner case where he is a co-defendant. The defendant's counsel, therefore, were quite right to advance his claim by way of counterclaim in the action; indeed, had they not done so, their client under the terms of paragraph (a) might have lost his right to claim contribution.

Paragraph (b) of subsection (1) requires that the third-party notice be served "as soon as is reasonably possible". The purpose behind this, according to McMahon J. in *A. & P. (Ireland) Ltd. v. Golden Vale Products Ltd*, unreported, High Court, December 7, 1978, was "to put the contributor in as good a position as possible in relation to knowledge of the claim and opportunity of investigating it." In *Gilmore v. Windle* [1967] I.R. 323, the plenary summons was issued on June 30, 1962 and the statement of claim was delivered on October 1, 1962. The application for leave to issue and serve the third-party notice was not brought until February 26, 1964. The delay was explained as occasioned by the fact that other similar applications were pending before the High Court and the defendant's advisors were awaiting an authoritative decision on the right to bring such proceedings before bringing their applications. In these circumstances the Supreme Court thought that the delay was not unreasonable.

In *Neville v. Margan Ltd*, unreported, High Court, December 1, 1988, however, proceedings were instituted against the defendant on June 29, 1978, and on February 23, 1981, the defendant obtained liberty to issue and serve a third-party notice out of the jurisdiction. The notice, however, was not served until July 22, 1983. Blayney J. said that the delay was wholly unreasonable and no explanation had been offered which might excuse it. The delay "clearly defeated" the purpose of putting the third-party in as good a position as possible in relation to knowledge of the claim and opportunity of investigating it. The delay also defeated the purpose of encouraging the bringing of claims for contribution by third-party proceedings and so having all questions arising for determination disposed of in a single proceeding: see O'Keeffe P. in *Gilmore v. Windle* [1967] I.R. 323 at 336. Since the third-party notice was not served until after the plaintiff's claim against the defendant had been settled on May 5, 1981, the claim for contribution was not different from what it would have been if it had been made in a separate independent action. Blayney J. therefore refused to make an order for contribution.

Similarly in *The Board of Governors of St Laurence's Hospital v. Staunton* [1990] 2 I.R. 31, Finlay C.J., with whom Hederman and McCarthy JJ. agreed, said that the first sentence in subsection (1)(b) created a definite obligation on a concurrent wrongdoer who is sued for damages and wishes to make a claim for contribution against a person not already a party to the action to do so by the service of a third-party notice as soon as was reasonably possible.

Here the plaintiff was injured in July 1981. He instituted proceedings against the hospital as sole defendant by plenary summons issued in September 1983. A statement of claim was filed in November 1983 and the hospital sought particulars which were eventually delivered in July 1984. A defence was filed in November 1984 and the action was set down in 1985. As a result of the trial in July 1987, the plaintiff obtained an award of £90,000 damages and the hospital appealed. After service of notice of appeal, the hospital served a notice of motion together with a third-party notice on the third-party in September 1987. Finlay C.J. said it was clear that the hospital were aware from July 1984 of the nature of the claim which was being brought against it:

> They may have been unaware as to whether that claim would succeed or not, but they were aware of what the nature of the claim was, and it must follow, it seems to me, that they were also aware at that time of any potential claim for contribution they might have against this third-party.

In those circumstances, serving a third-party notice after the conclusion of the plaintiff's claim was not serving it as soon as was reasonably possible.

It is clear from these decisions, and subsequent ones such as *O'Brien v. Ulster Bank Ltd*, unreported, High Court, December 21, 1993 (a delay of 15 months), *Dillon v. MacGabhann*, unreported, High Court, July 24, 1995 and *SFL Engineering Ltd v. Smyth Cladding Systems Ltd*, unreported, High Court, May 9, 1997 (both delays of 22 months), that the words "as soon as is reasonably possible" in section 27(1)(b) denote that there should be as little delay as possible. The use of the word "reasonable", however, indicates, as Barron J. observed in *McElwaine v. Hughes*, unreported, High Court, April 30, 1997, "that circumstances may exist which justify some delay in the bringing of proceedings". All the elements which contributed to any possible delay in effecting service have to be considered. For Barron J., the real question hinged upon "what is reasonable in the particular case" which, in turn, depended upon the behaviour of the defendant's advisors:

> The first question to be determined is at what point in time would a reasonably prudent solicitor acting for the defendant be in a position to advise the institution of third-party proceedings. Then if such proceedings are not instituted at that time, the further question that may arise, was such delay or such further delay reasonable?
>
> In my opinion a defendant is entitled to decide first, whether the proceedings should be defended and, if so, on what basis. This in an appropriate case would involve a decision whether to institute third-party proceedings. Such time should be allowed as is reasonably necessary to reach such decisions and to obtain such evidence as may be required upon which to base them. Once, acting within these parameters, there is sufficient evidence upon which to base such decisions, then that is the time at which the solicitor will be in a position to give the appropriate advice. If the solicitor then delays to get further evidence for some purpose other than that of reaching such decisions such further delay would be unreasonable. When referring to the solicitor I also include time taken to obtain Counsel's advice where Counsel is instructed.

In this case, the plaintiff's claim was for damages for negligence and breach of duty arising out of the consumption of shellfish at the defendant's hotel. The statement of claim was delivered in July 1993 and, although the defendant sought further and better particulars in September and October 1993, it was clear "from an early stage in the proceedings" that the oysters consumed by the plaintiff were isolated as being the cause of his personal injuries. It was not until the replies to the notices for particulars were furnished in April 1994, however, that confirmation was received by the defendant that the plaintiff was relying on the oysters as the cause of his injuries. On receipt of these replies the defendant's solicitor was advised by counsel to seek the opinion of a microbiologist and that opinion was eventually received in January 1995. Having received this opinion, a defence was filed 12 days later and a notice of motion for liberty to serve a third-party notice was issued on February 21, 1995.

Barron J. accepted that, once the defence had been delivered, albeit late, proceedings were brought within a reasonable time for liberty to serve the third-party notice. He did not want to suggest, however, that a defendant should be able to rely upon the delay in the delivery of a defence to justify delay in the institution of third-party proceedings "since the third-party procedure can be set in motion at any time and without reference to the delivery of a defence". What was important was "the time reasonably taken to decide upon the manner in which the proceedings should be met including the institution of third-party proceedings" and, in the present case, he was satisfied that those proceedings were sought as soon as reasonably possible (see also Morris J. in *Dowling v. Armour Pharmaceutical Co. Inc.* [1996] 2 I.L.R.M. 417).

Barron J. also made the point that, although the wording of the section referred to the *service* of the third-party notice, it seemed to him that, unless there were circumstances arising between the issue of the application to issue and serve a third-party notice and its ultimate service following an order to that effect, "the time to be considered should end at the date of issue of the application to the Court". Morris J., however, in *Dillon v. MacGabhan*, unreported, High Court, July 24, 1995 was of the view that the court should look to the date upon which the third-party notice was served. In so far as there is a conflict between the views of Barron and Morris JJ., Kelly J. in *Connolly v. Casey*, unreported, High Court, June 12, 1998, preferred that of Morris J., "since it accords precisely with the wording of the section". Furthermore, Morris J. was of the opinion that since the obligation was on the defendant to serve the notice within a reasonable time, the onus of proof of showing that the delay, if delay there was, not unreasonably lay upon the defendant. The view that the onus of proof lies upon the defendant was shared by Kelly J. in *Connolly v. Casey*, unreported, High Court, June 12, 1998.

The Supreme Court in *Staunton* also held that it was not the case that a concurrent wrongdoer sued for damages who wished to make a claim against a person not already a party to the action could only do so by the service of a third-party notice in accordance with section 27(1)(b). If he failed to serve such a notice, he could still proceed by substantive action in a claim for contribution brought by civil bill or plenary summons. If this were not so, the second sentence in the subsection would be superfluous:

> If the only method of making the claim for contribution was by the service of a third-party notice in the action then there would be no necessity to make any provision for the consequence of failure to serve a third-party notice in accordance with the first sentence in the sub-section for its only conceivable result would be that the claim for contribution could not be made.

Any substantive claim for contribution is brought subject to the proviso that, the defendant having failed to serve a third-party notice in the action, there is vested in the court a discretion to refuse to make an order for contribution in his favour, even if it were satisfied that he could establish a right to contribution on the facts presented to it. Finlay C.J., said it seemed clear that this discretion was:

> . . . part of the general policy of the provisions of the Act of 1961 seeking to have all claims determined at the same time and is also a potential protection to a person against whom a claim for contribution is made against unfair or prejudicial procedure.

Subsection (5) was inserted by section 3 of the Civil Liability (Amendment) Act 1964 and was prompted in part by the decision of Murnaghan J. in *Gilmore v. Windle*, unreported,

High Court, April 10, 1964. Here the plaintiff was injured when he was struck by the defendant's motor car. The plaintiff issued and served on the defendant a plenary summons claiming damages and alleging that the defendant had been negligent in the driving of her car. The defendant had purchased the car two days before the accident and she claimed that it had been represented to her by the vendor that the car was in a sound mechanical condition, that the accident had occurred by reason of a sudden and total failure of the brakes and that she was entitled to claim from the vendor a contribution towards . . . or an indemnity against any damages which she might be compelled to pay to the plaintiff. She therefore applied to the High Court for leave to issue and serve a third-party notice on the vendor pursuant to section 27(1). This application was refused on the ground that the defendant had not conceded that she was a wrongdoer within the meaning of section 27. The defendant appealed, and before the hearing of the appeal, section 27 was amended by the insertion of subsection (5). Before the Supreme Court (whose judgment is reported at [1967] I.R. 323) counsel for the intended third-party conceded that the enactment was procedural and therefore retrospective in effect. The Supreme Court, however, unanimously held that even if subsection (5) had not been inserted the Court still had jurisdiction to bring in the vendor under what is now Rules of the Superior Courts 1986, Ord. 16, r. 1 which permits of third-party proceedings in a much wider class of cases than section 27(1). (This decision was followed in *Mullen v. Doyle*, unreported, Supreme Court, May 10, 1967.) As Costello J. said in *Staunton v. Toyota (Ireland) Ltd*, unreported, High Court, April 15, 1988:

> The Rules make available to defendants third-party procedures not just for statutory claims for contribution or indemnity under the Civil Liability Act 1961 but also for non-statutory claims arising otherwise than under the Act.

The Rules of the Superior Courts 1986, Ord. 16, r. 1 provide where a defendant claims, against any person not already a party to the action (referred to in the Order as the third-party):

    (a)   that he is entitled to contribution or indemnity, or

    (b)   that he is entitled to any relief or remedy relating to or connected with the original subject matter of the action and substantially the same as some relief or remedy claimed by the plaintiff, or,

    (c)   that any question or issue relating to or connected with the said subject matter is substantially the same as some question or issue arising between the plaintiff and the defendant and should properly be determined not only as between the plaintiff and the defendant but as between the plaintiff and the defendant and the third-party or between any or either of them, then the Court may give leave to issue and serve a third-party notice.

Ord. 16, r. 1(3) of the Rules of the Superior Courts 1986 provides that application for leave to issue a third-party notice, unless otherwise ordered by the court, shall be made within 28 days from the time limited for delivering the defence. In *Golden Vale plc v. Food Industries plc* [1996] 2 I.R. 221 at 227, McCracken J. commented that, in his experience, "this is a provision which is frequently breached", although in that case he was prepared to make an order extending the time.

It is the practice that where an application is made under Ord. 16, r. 1 for leave to serve a third-party notice, and where the court gives leave, liberty is reserved to the proposed third-party named in the notice to apply to the court to set the order aside. Any such application should be brought before "significant costs and expenses have been incurred in the third-party procedure" (*per* Morris J. in *Carroll v. Fulflex International Co. Ltd*, unreported, High Court, October 18, 1995) and, save in exceptional circumstances, should not extend "beyond the point where a defence is delivered to the third-party statement of claim" (*per* Morris J. in both *Tierney v. Fintan Sweeney Ltd*, unreported, High Court, October 18, 1995 and *Grogan v. Ferrum Trading Co. Ltd* [1996] 2 I.L.R.M. 216).

In considering whether an order joining a third-party should be set aside, is the court concerned with any question of prejudice arising as a result of the delay in applying for liberty to join the third-party? In *SFL Engineering Ltd v. Smyth Cladding Systems Ltd*, unreported, High Court, May 9, 1997, Kelly J. was emphatic that the question of prejudice was not something with which he ought to be concerned. See also his judgment in *Connolly v. Casey*, unreported, High Court, June 12, 1998. In *Ward v. O'Callaghan*, unreported, High Court, February 2, 1998, however, the defendant served the third-party notice approximately 16 months after the time limit prescribed by the Rules of the Superior Courts 1986 had expired. Morris P. was of the view that, although the defendant had clearly failed to comply with the Rules, the delay, standing alone, would not be of such significance as to constitute a ground for setting aside the third-party procedure. To constitute such a ground "it would be necessary for the delay of this length to be coupled with circumstances which amounted to a prejudice suffered by the third-party based on this delay". Morris P. did point out, however, that it was agreed between the parties that the third-party was not a concurrent wrongdoer with the defendant and accordingly section 27(1)(b) of the 1961 Act had no application.

The Supreme Court has ruled in *Johnston v. Fitzpatrick* [1992] I.L.R.M. 269, that there is no inflexible rule that an application for liberty to issue and serve a third-party notice must be based on a direct affidavit of the facts, rather than on an "information and belief" affidavit. There will be circumstances, however, where the former will be necessary (see *D'Arcy v. Roscommon County Council*, unreported, Supreme Court, January 11, 1991). In *Johnston* Egan J. (with whom Hederman, McCarthy and O'Flaherty JJ. agreed) emphasised that, in an application under Ord. 16, the defendant must allege facts which would support the claim that the proposed third-party had contributed to the accident. Finlay C.J., however, pointed out that it had not been contended by the defendant that he was not obliged to establish a stateable or *prima facie* right to a claim against the proposed third-party and he deliberately expressed no view on whether such an onus rested on a defendant seeking to add a third-party by leave of the court.

Assuming the court accepts that the proposed third-party might have been guilty of a want of care which contributed to the accident, what other issues arise with regard to the exercise by the court of the discretion which it has under Ord. 16, r. 1? In *Quirke v. O'Shea* [1992] I.L.R.M. 286, it was submitted that the only other issue which could arise is the question as to whether the issue with regard to liability between the plaintiff and the defendant is sufficiently similar and close to the issue with regard to liability between the defendant and the proposed third-party as to make it convenient that both issues should be tried in the one action. The Supreme Court (Finlay C.J., Hederman and Egan JJ.) were satisfied, however, that the discretion was not so confined. The Chief Justice said that in the case of a claim by an infant plaintiff suing by a parent and next friend, where an application is made to add that next friend as a third-party, the court was entitled "to balance the disruption to the existing proceedings which could arise from such joinder against the convenience of trying all the issues in the one action". So, in *Hallahan v. Keane and Harrington* [1992] I.L.R.M. 595, O'Hanlon J. refused the second-named defendant's application to join the infant plaintiff's father and next friend as a third-party, even though there were reasonable grounds for that defendant wishing to maintain a claim for contribution or indemnity, because of the father's very limited means. As O'Hanlon J. went on to expressly point out, however, the refusal was without prejudice to the second-named defendant's entitlement to bring separate proceedings against the father seeking contribution or indemnity, should he elect to do so.

Third-party procedures in the District Court are governed by Ord. 42 of the District Court Rules 1997 (S.I. No. 93 of 1997) (see Appendix Two, page 87).

What if the prospective third-party is not within the jurisdiction? Can leave be granted to serve the third-party notice out of the jurisdiction? The question was considered in *International Commercial Bank plc v. Insurance Corporation of Ireland* [1989] I.L.R.M. 788.

In the High Court, Costello J. pointed out that, although Ord. 16 contained no provision for service out of the jurisdiction, Ord. 11 did. Having given a list of circumstances in which service of a summons out of the jurisdiction might be granted the order then provides in rule 11 that "this Order shall apply, so far as practicable and applicable, to proceedings whether instituted by originating summons or in some other manner, and to any order or notice in any such proceedings". Rule 1 sets out different circumstances in which a summons out of the jurisdiction can be serviced and paragraph (h) provides that leave to issue a summons out of the jurisdiction will be granted when "any person out of the jurisdiction is a necessary or proper party to an action properly brought against some person duly served within the jurisdiction." Costello J. accepted the defendant's argument that this rule was made applicable to third-party notices by the Rules of the Superior Courts 1986, Ord. 11, r. 11.

The defendant, however, still had to show that the prospective third-party was a "proper party" to the action. It did not suffice, said Costello J.:

> for a defendant to show that the claim against the foreign domiciliary falls within the rules relating to the issue of third-party notices; it must also be shown that it is proper in all the circumstances of the case to order service out of the jurisdiction of the third-party notice.

The decision of Costello J. was upheld by the Supreme Court. Finlay C.J., with whom Griffin and McCarthy JJ. agreed, said:

> The modern development of procedures against third parties in respect of claims for contribution or indemnity . . . indicates a clear recognition by the courts of the requirement of justice which so frequently involves the necessity as far as possible to ensure that a party against whom a claim has been made and who has legal rights against some other party which may relieve him from some or even all of the consequences of that claim should be entitled to have the issue of his liability and of his consequential rights determined in a single set of proceedings and as far as possible at the same time.

In the absence of a clear provision to the contrary he felt obliged to interpret Ord. 11, r. 1(h) with regard to service out of the jurisdiction "so as to comply with that fair procedure concerning third-party claims."

Leave to serve a third-party notice is usually given on an *ex parte* application and before the defence is filed. It can be applied for, however, on notice to the plaintiff and co-defendants. The usual form of the order is that:

> the Third Party be at liberty to appear at the trial of this Action and to take such part therein as the trial judge shall direct and be bound by the result of the trial and that the question of the liability herein of the Third Party to make contribution to or to indemnify the Defence be tried at or after the trial of the Action as the Judge shall direct.

As Costello J. pointed out in *Staunton v. Toyota (Ireland) Ltd*, unreported, High Court, April 15, 1988, such an order "has the merit of saving the expense of a second application for directions".

On the question of a third-party's costs, the Rules of the Superior Courts 1986, Ord. 16, r. 10 provide that the court may decide all questions of costs as between a third-party and the other parties to the action and may order any one or more to pay the costs of any other or others or give such directions as to costs as the justice of the case may require.

Distribution of loss on failure to obtain satisfaction

28.—Where, of three or more concurrent wrongdoers, judgment for contribution is given in favour of one against two or more, the claimant, at any time within the period limited by law for the enforcement of judgments and upon proof that, after taking reasonable steps, he has failed to obtain satisfaction of any judgment in whole or in part, shall have liberty to apply for secondary judgments having the effect of distributing the deficiency among the other defendants in such proportions as may be just and equitable.

GENERAL NOTE

This section provides for the distribution of loss caused by failure to obtain satisfaction from one of three or more concurrent wrongdoers.

Estoppel when contribution is claimed

29.—(1) In any proceeding for contribution, the contributor shall not be entitled to resist the claim on the ground that the claimant who has paid the injured person was not liable to such person; but, subject to this section and to the general law of estoppel, he may resist the claim on the ground that he himself is not liable to such person and, for this purpose, may dispute any question of law or fact even though that question arises also on the liability of the claimant to the injured person; and the contributor may in the same way dispute the amount of the damage suffered by the injured person.

(2) Where a claim for contribution is made by third-party notice in the injured person's action and the third-party is given leave to defend the main action, he shall be bound by the finding of the court upon the questions that he is given leave to defend.

(3) Where the contributor had knowledge of an action brought by the injured person against the claimant, and unreasonably failed to make a proposal for assisting the claimant in the defence of the action, and the injured person obtained judgment against the claimant, the contributor shall, in any proceeding brought against him by the claimant, be estopped from disputing the propriety or amount of the judgment obtained by the injured person or any question of law or fact common to the claimant's liability to the injured person and the contributor's liability to the injured person: but the contributor shall not be so estopped where the claimant submitted to judgment in fraud of the contributor.

(4) In any proceeding for contribution the claimant shall be bound by any finding of law or fact in the injured person's action against him that was necessary to establish his liability to the injured person.

(5) Where the injured person has sued the claimant and contributor together and failed against the contributor, the claimant shall, in any proceeding for contribution, be bound by any finding of law or fact that was necessary to negative the contributor's liability to the injured person: provided that—

    (a) the claimant shall not be so bound where the injured person submitted to judgment in fraud of the claimant;

    (b) this subsection shall not apply where the injured person's action was brought in a court outside the State, unless by the law of the court the claimant had an opportunity of presenting evidence against the contributor, of appealing against a judgment in his favour and of contesting an appeal by him.

(6) (a) A decision on the proportion of fault between claimant and contributor on a claim for contribution shall be binding upon the same persons in a subsequent claim in respect of damage suffered by one or both of them arising out of the same facts, and, conversely, such a decision in a claim in respect of such damage shall be binding upon the same persons in a subsequent claim for contribution.

    (b) Paragraph (a) of this subsection shall apply between two parties notwithstanding that one of them is party to the two actions in different capacities.

(7) A concurrent wrongdoer who makes a payment to the injured person without action in settlement of the injured person's claim against himself and

who subsequently claims contribution under section 22 shall, where the injured person has sued the contributor, be bound by the apportionment made by the court in the injured person's action in accordance with paragraph (h) of subsection (1) of section 35.

(8) It shall not be a defence to a claim for contribution merely to show that the injured person has failed in an action against the contributor to which the claimant was not a party.

GENERAL NOTE

This section deals with estoppel where contribution is claimed. According to the Explanatory Memorandum accompanying the Bill, subsection (1) should be read in conjunction with section 16(4) and establishes estoppel for the benefit of a stranger who sues for contribution. Although the contributor will not be entitled to resist the claim on the ground that the claimant was not liable to the injured person, the contributor will not be estopped from disputing his own liability to the injured person on the amount of the damage suffered by the injured person.

Subsection (2) provides that, where a third-party brought in on a claim for contribution by third-party notice is given leave to defend the main action by the injured person, he or she shall be bound by the findings of the court upon the questions he or she is given leave to defend. This also allows the third-party to appeal from a judgment given in favour of the plaintiff.

Subsection (3) creates an estoppel in respect of questions common to the liability of the claimant and the contributor where the contributor knew of the action by the injured person against the claimant and unreasonably failed to make a proposal for assisting the claimant's defence. According to the Explanatory Memorandum accompanying the Bill, the object of the subsection is to avoid as far as possible completely new trials of issues already litigated.

Subsection (4) involves an extension of the *res judicata* rule by preventing the claimant from disputing in the contribution proceedings any findings of law or fact already made in the injured person's action against him or her.

Subsection (5) applies the *res judicata* rule in contribution proceedings where the injured person has already sued the claimant and the contributor together and failed against the contributor, unless:

(i) the injured person submitted to judgment in fraud of the claimant, or
(ii) the injured person's action was brought in a court outside the State and the claimant under the *lex fori* had no opportunity of presenting evidence against the contributor, of appealing against judgment in his or her favour, and of contesting an appeal by the contributor.

The English Law Commission in Working Paper No. 59, *Contribution* (1975) were of the view, at 23, that a case could be made for allowing D1 to reopen the question of D2's liability to P for the purpose of contribution proceedings even when D2 has defeated P's claim on the merits. The example given was where D1, unknown to P, had vital evidence of D2's liability in his possession and P's claim against D2 fails for the lack of it. Should D1 then, in accordance with section 35(1)(j), be able to use that evidence to reduce the amount of his own liability?

Subsection (6) provides that where there are separate proceedings between concurrent wrongdoers, whether for contribution or in respect of their own injuries, the decision on the proportion of fault arrived at in the first proceedings will be binding in the second proceedings.

Subsection (7) deals with the case where one concurrent wrongdoer (D1) settles with the injured person (P) and then claims contribution against another wrongdoer (D2) after P has sued D2. D1 will be bound by any apportionment made in P. action against D2.

Subsection (8) provides that it is not a defence to a claim contribution merely to show that the injured person has failed in an action against the contributor to which the claimant was not a party.

Legal incidents of claim for contribution

30.—The right to ask the court for an award of contribution shall be deemed to be in the nature of a quasi-contractual right which shall pass to the personal representatives of the claimant for the benefit of his estate, and shall avail against the personal representatives of the contributor; and the right to contribution shall be deemed to be a cause of action within section 9.

GENERAL NOTE

This section is concerned with the legal incidents of a claim for contribution and provides that the right to seek contribution shall be deemed to be a quasi-contractual right; the term "quasi contract", according to the Explanatory Memorandum accompanying the Bill, is "conveniently used to cover every case of restitution consequent upon unjust enrichment, whether the restitution stems from common law or statute".

Limitation of actions for contribution

31.—An action may be brought for contribution within the same period as the injured person is allowed by law for bringing an action against the contributor, or within the period of two years after the liability of the claimant is ascertained or the injured person's damages are paid, whichever is the greater.

GENERAL NOTE

This section provides that where one concurrent wrongdoer seeks contribution from another concurrent wrongdoer the action for contribution may be brought either within the same period as the injured person is allowed by law for bringing an action against the contributor or within the period of two years after the liability of the claimant is ascertained or the injured person's damages are paid, whichever is the greater. In *Buckley v. Lynch* [1987] I.R. 6 Finlay P. (as he then was) held that a claim for contribution made by the third-party procedure was "an action for contribution within the meaning of section 31". This section clears up the prior conflict of judicial opinion as to the period of limitation relating to claims for contribution or indemnities.

In cases such as *Littlewood v. George Wimpey & Co. Ltd* [1953] 2 Q.B. 501, *Brambles Construction Pty Ltd v. Helmers* (1966) 114 C.L.R. 213, *Re Urquhart and Hatt* (1982) 132 D.L.R. (3d) 685 and *Van Win Pty Ltd v. Eleventh Mirontron Pty Ltd* [1986] V.R. 484, it was held that time did not begin to run in favour of a third-party until the liability of the defendant was ascertained, it being only then that the right to claim contribution arose. In *Merlihan v. A.C. Pope Ltd* [1946] 1 K.B. 106, however, it had been held that time began to run from the date of the wrongful act.

Section 31 now provides for three alternative dates as to when time commences, but, as Blayney J. pointed out in *Neville v. Margan Ltd*, unreported, High Court, December 1, 1988, it only provides for two alternative limitation periods. The first is the period the injured person had for bringing an action against the contributor and the second is whichever of two periods of two years is appropriate on the facts. If the liability of the claimant is ascertained by a judgment or a settlement the period would be two years from the date of the judgment or settlement; if, on the other hand, the claimant has paid to the injured party "a sum on account of his damages" as is envisaged by section 22, or has paid a reasonable consideration for a release or accord, which under section 22 is to be treated as a payment of damages, then the period of two years would run from the date of the payment of the damages or the date of the release or accord.

In *Neville*, Blayney J. continued as follows:

> Where a claimant's liability has been ascertained by a judgment or settlement, it seems logical that his cause of action against the contributor should be held to

accrue then as he is at once in a position to formulate his claim against the contributor. And it seems wholly illogical that the claimant, by failing to pay the damages, should be able to extend the period he has for claiming against the contributor.

Blayney J. concluded by saying it did not follow that as long as a claim was made within the period laid down by section 31 it would automatically be allowed. So to hold would be to disregard the "plain words" of section 27 (which requires that the application be made a soon as is reasonably possible) and make that section a nullity.

Section 31 applies equally to claims for contribution or indemnity arising out of an action in tort or contract: *per* Wild C.J. in *Wrightcel (New Zealand) Ltd v. Felvin Suppliers and Distributors Ltd* [1975] N.Z.L.R. 50 at 53. Note, however, that section 23(4) provides that a payment of damages by the claimant for contribution, at a time when the injured person's cause of action against the claimant is barred by the Statute of Limitations 1957, or any other limitation enactment, shall not found a claim to levy execution under a judgment for contribution. Note also that section 44 provides that where, in any claim for contribution between wrongdoers, the defendant avoids liability to the plaintiff by pleading the Statute of Limitations neither he nor any other person responsible for his acts shall be entitled to recover any damages or contribution from the plaintiff.

Evidence and appeals

32.—(1) Where an action is brought against two or more persons as concurrent wrongdoers, each defendant shall have the right to present evidence against the other or others.

(2) Where an action is brought against two or more persons as concurrent wrongdoers and the plaintiff obtains judgment and the judgment is satisfied by one of such wrongdoers, another of such wrongdoers may appeal against the judgment notwithstanding that it has been satisfied

(3) Where an action is brought against two or more persons as concurrent wrongdoers and the plaintiff obtains judgment and one defendant appeals against the judgment, another defendant may, upon giving such notice as may be required by rules of court, contest the appeal as respondent.

(4) Where an action is brought against two or more persons as concurrent wrongdoers and the plaintiff succeeds against one and fails against another, the unsuccessful defendant may appeal against the judgment in favour of the successful defendant.

GENERAL NOTE

This section, which appears to do no more than state the existing law, is necessary to allow claims for contribution as between the defendants to be disposed of in the plaintiff's action. The Rules of the Superior Courts 1986, Ord. 58, r. 22 (appeals to Supreme Court) and Ord. 61, r. 10 (appeals from the Circuit Court) provide that, where a defendant desires to contest as respondent, in pursuance of subsection (3), an appeal brought by a co-defendant, he or she must serve notice of intention to do so "upon such co-defendant and the plaintiff and upon any other party directly affected thereby, within seven days from the date on which the notice of appeal was served upon him [or her], or within such extended time as may be allowed" and, further, that he or she should lodge a copy of the notice of intention to contest the appeal with the Registrar of the Supreme Court or the County Registrar (as appropriate) "at latest upon the day after the last service of such notice" (Appendix Three, page 95).

Contribution to be regarded as damages

33.—(1) For the purpose of a contract issuing against liability for a wrong or against a liability to pay damages, the liability of a wrongdoer to make contribution under this Part to a concurrent wrongdoer shall be deemed to be a liability to pay damages for a wrong, unless the contrary intention appears from the contract.

(2) Where a claim for contribution between wrongdoers is made under a contract for contribution between them, the provisions of subsection (1) of this section shall apply to the extent that the claim could have been made under the provisions of this Part A instead of under the contract for contribution.

GENERAL NOTE

This section makes it clear that the statutory liability to pay contribution will be regarded as coming within the terms of an insurance policy against liability to pay damages for a wrong unless a contrary intention appears from the insurance contract. The purpose of subsection (2), according to the Explanatory Memorandum accompanying the Bill, is that where the claim for contribution is made under a contribution contract between the wrongdoers, the assured wrongdoer will have a right of indemnity against the insurance company only to the extent that he would have been statutorily liable for contribution, "The idea is to limit the insurer's risk where the assured makes a secret contract for contribution with his fellow-wrongdoer."

CHAPTER III

Contributory Negligence

Apportionment of liability in case of contributory negligence

34.—(1) Where, in any action brought by one person in respect of a wrong committed by any other person, it is proved that the damage suffered by the plaintiff was caused partly by the negligence or want of care of the plaintiff or of one for whose acts he is responsible (in this Part called contributory negligence) and partly by the wrong of the defendant, the damages recoverable in respect of the said wrong shall be reduced by such amount as, the court thinks just and equitable having regard to the degrees of fault of the plaintiff and defendant: provided that—

    (a) if, having regard to all the circumstances of the case, it is not possible to establish different degrees of fault, the liability shall be apportioned equally;

    (b) this subsection shall not operate to defeat any defence arising under a contract or the defence that the plaintiff before the act complained of agreed to waive his legal rights in respect of it, whether or not for value; but, subject as aforesaid, the provisions of this subsection shall apply notwithstanding that the defendant might, apart from this subsection, have the defence of voluntary assumption of risk;

    (c) where any contract or enactment providing for the limitation of liability is applicable to the claim, the amount of damages awarded to the plaintiff by virtue of his subsection shall not exceed the maximum limit so applicable.

(2) For the purpose of subsection (1) of this section—

    (a) damage suffered by the plaintiff may include damages paid by the plaintiff to a third person who has suffered damage owing to the concurrent wrongs of the plaintiff and the defendant, and the period of limitation for claiming such damages shall be the same as is provided by section 31 for actions for contribution;

(b) a negligent or careless failure to mitigate damage shall be deemed to be contributory negligence in respect of the amount by which such damage exceeds the damage that would otherwise have occurred;

(c) the plaintiff's failure to exercise reasonable care for his own protection shall not amount to contributory negligence in respect of damage unless that damage results from the particular risk to which his conduct has exposed him, and the plaintiff's breach of statutory duty shall not amount to contributory negligence unless the damage of which he complains is damage that the statute was designed to prevent;

(d) the plaintiff's failure to exercise reasonable care in the protection of his own property shall, except to the extent that the defendant has been unjustly enriched, be deemed to be contributory negligence in an action for conversion of the property;

(e) damage may be held to be caused by the wrong of the defendant notwithstanding any rule of law by which the scope of the defendant's duty is limited to cases where the plaintiff has not been guilty of contributory negligence: but this paragraph shall not render the defendant liable for any damage in respect of which he or a person for whose acts he is responsible has not been careless in fact;

(f) where an action is brought for negligence in respect of a thing that has caused damage, the fact that there was a reasonable possibility or probability of examination after the thing had left the hands of the defendant shall not, by itself exclude the defendant's duty, but may be taken as evidence that he was not in the circumstances negligent in parting with the thing in its dangerous state.

(3) Article 21 of the Warsaw Convention (which empowers a court to exonerate wholly or partly a carrier who proves that the damage was caused by or contributed to by the negligence of the injured person) shall have effect subject to the provisions of this Part.

GENERAL NOTE

This section provides for apportionment of liability according to the degree each party is at fault. At common law, the rule was that if there was blame causing the accident on both sides, however small that blame might be on one side, the loss lay where it fell: *per* Lord Blackburn in *Cayzer, Irvine & Co. v. Carron Co.* (1884) 9 App. Cas. 873 at 881. The harshness of this penal rule led to the development of the last clear chance or last opportunity rule, developments which ensured that contributory negligence was one of the most difficult branches of the law involving "subtle arguments and tedious refinements".

Indeed, the doctrine of "last clear chance" was described by Picard J.A., giving the judgment of the Alberta Court of Appeal in *Wickberg v. Patterson* (1997) 145 D.L.R. (4th) 263 at 266, as "the dandelion of causation analysis". Section 34, once described by Murnaghan J. (SYS lecture No. 36, November 3, 1968) as the "most important provision in the Act", rationalises the law by enabling the court to reduce the damages recoverable by such amount as it thinks just and equitable, having regard to the degrees of fault of the plaintiff and defendant. This new procedure, said Murnaghan J., was an "immense improvement" on the previous one. It is also much more rational. In a system in which liability is based on fault, the extent of fault should govern the extent of liability: see Sullivan J. in *Li v. Yellow Cab Company* (1975) 532 P. 2d. 1226 at 1231. It should be noted that apportionment of loss already applied to cases of collisions at sea by virtue of section 1 of the Maritime Conventions Act 1911.

Because the section refers to the fault of the plaintiff and defendant, it would seem to follow that, in order for any degree of fault to be attributed to a person, such person must be a party to the action in some way. In other words, if the court allocates 20 per cent of the blame to the plaintiff, 40 per cent to the defendant and 40 per cent to a person or persons not party to the action, judgment should he entered against the defendant for 80 per cent not 40 per cent of the loss. See the contrary decision of the British Columbia Court of Appeal in *Wells v. McBrine* (1988) 54 D.L.R. (4th) 708 where the relevant apportionment legislation provided:

> Where by the fault of two or more persons damage or loss is caused to one or more of them, the liability to make good the damage or loss shall be in proportion to the degree in which each person was at fault.

Unlike the question of negligence there need not be any breach of duty. All the defendant has to do is to show that the plaintiff failed to take reasonable care for his own safety in respect of the particular danger which in fact occurred. A passenger in a car who fails to wear a seatbelt is not thereby in breach of any duty to the defendant but may be held guilty of contributory negligence: see *Hamill v. Oliver* [1977] I.R. 73 and *Froom v. Butcher* [1976] Q.B. 286; likewise for motor cyclists and crash helmets see *O'Connell v. Jackson* [1972] 1 Q.B. 270 and *Capps v. Miller* [1989] 1 W.L.R. 839. *Quaere* whether there is an obligation on the drivers to exhort passengers to wear a seat belt? In *Eastman v. South West Thames Regional Health Authority* [1991] RTR 389 at 393, Russell L.J. said that in the absence of very special circumstances, such as the infancy of the plaintiff, there was no such duty.

Where the defence of contributory negligence is raised, the onus of proof lies on the party alleging the contributory negligence and he or she must offer positive evidence of same: see *Wilson v. McGrath*, unreported, High Court, Flood J., January 17, 1996.

The two leading cases are *O'Sullivan v. Dwyer* [1971] I.R. 275 and *Carroll v. Clare County Council* [1975] I.R. 221. In the former, Walsh J. (Ó Dálaigh C.J. and Fitzgerald J. concurring) said that there was a distinction between 'causation,' and 'fault', and that degrees of fault between the parties were not to be "apportioned on the basis of the relative causative potency of their respective causative contributions to the damage, but rather on the basis of the moral blameworthiness of their respective causative contributions." There were limits to this, he continued at 286, since fault was not to be measured by purely subjective standards:

> Blameworthiness is to be measured against the degree of capacity or knowledge which such a person ought to have had if he were an ordinary reasonable person.

This was elaborated upon by Kenny J. (Henchy and Griffin JJ. concurring) in the latter case. He thought that 'fault' in section 34 meant "a departure from a norm by a person who, as a result of such departure, has been found to have been negligent" and that 'degrees of fault' expressed "the extent of his departure from the standard of behaviour to be expected from a reasonable man or woman in the circumstances". Kenny J. also said that he thought the use of the word 'moral' in connection with blameworthiness was likely to mislead. In his view, the extent of departure from the norm was not to be measured by moral considerations, for to do so would introduce a subjective element into what was surely an objective test:

> It is the blameworthiness, by reference to what a reasonable man or woman would have done in the circumstances, of the contributions of the plaintiff and defendant to the happening of the accident which is to be the basis of the apportionment.

So in *Hamill v. Oliver* [1977] I.R. 73 Griffin J. said at 76:

> Any person who travels in the front seat of a motor car, be he passenger or driver,

without wearing an available seat belt must normally be held guilty of contributory negligence if the injuries in respect of which he sues were caused wholly or in part as a result of his failure to wear a seat-belt.

The learned judge did indicate, however, that there might be excusing circumstances for failure to wear a seat belt "such as obesity, pregnancy, post-operative convalescence, and the like, where the wearing of a seat belt might be thought to do more harm than good".

The "comparative blameworthiness" approach is criticised by White, *op. cit.* at pp. 36–37 and 41–44 who prefers the "deviation" approach (see Payne (1955) 18 M.L.R. 344 and Gravells (1977) 93 L.Q.R. 581). This approach is said to involve ignoring the basis of the defendant's liability and holding him responsible for all of the plaintiff's damage except that part of it which is attributable to the plaintiff's negligence. On this basis, the damages are reduced having regard to the extent of the plaintiff's deviation, expressed as a percentage, from the standard of care of the reasonable person and without reference to the blameworthiness, or want of it, attributable to the defendant.

When dealing with children, the test is not that of an experienced adult but what may be expected having regard to the child's age and mental development. In *Fleming v. Kerry County Council* [1955–56] Ir. Jur. Rep. 71 at 72, O'Byrne J. said:

> In the case of a child of tender years there must be some age up to which the child cannot be guilty of contributory negligence. In other words, there is some age up to which a child cannot be expected to take any precaution for his own safety. In cases where contributory negligence is alleged against a child, it is the duty of the trial judge to rule, in each particular case, whether the plaintiff, having regard to his age and mental development, may properly be expected to take some precautions for his own safety and consequently be capable of being guilty of contributory negligence.

See also *Duffy v. Fahy* [1960] Ir. Jur. Rep. 69 and McMahon and Binchy, *Irish Law of Torts* (2nd, ed., 1990) at pp. 715–722.

The section applies to any "wrongdoer" including those guilty of breach of contract (*per* Pringle J. in. *Bewley Ryan & Company v. Cruess-Callaghan*, unreported, High Court, January 16, 1974 at 31 and *per* Griffin J. in *McCord v. Electricity Supply Board* [1980] I.L.R.M. 153 at 165) or breach of trust (*per* Henry J. in *Fletcher v. National Mutual Life Nominees Ltd* [1990] 1 N.Z.L.R. 97 at 107). It is also clear, given the definition of 'wrong' as meaning a "tort . . . whether or not . . . intentional", that it would also apply to cases where the defence was not available at common law. On the issue of whether contributory negligence is available at common law to intentional torts such as inducement of breach of contract, conspiracy, assault, battery, or deceit, see *Dellabarca v. Northern Storemen and Packers Union* [1989] 2 N.Z.L.R. 734 at 757, *per* Smellie J. saying that it was not available; *Hoebergen v. Koppens* [1974] 2 N.Z.L.R. 597 at 601–602, *per* Moller J. saying it was, and *Alliance & Leicester Building Society v. Edgestop Ltd* [1993] 1 W.L.R. 1462 at 1477, *per* Mummery J. saying it was not. See also Hudson (1984) 4 Legal Studies 332.

Whether section 34 permitted the negativing of annulment of damages recoverable as well as their reduction was considered by the Supreme Court in *McCord v. Electricity Supply Board* [1980] I.L.R.M. 153. O'Higgins C.J. said, at 158, that it only authorised the reduction of such damages, but the other judges (Henchy, Griffin, Kenny and Parke JJ.) felt that the fault of the plaintiff, in unreasonably refusing to comply with a reasonable request, so outweighed the fault of the defendant that, in their opinion, justice and equity required that the entire of the damage should lie upon the plaintiff. See also the *ex tempore* judgment of Morris J. in *Felloni v. Dublin Corporation* [1998] 1 I.L.R.M. 133. Note, however, the view of the English Court of Appeal (Dillon, Balcombe and Beldam L.JJ.), in *Pitts v. Hunt* [1991] 1 Q.B. 24, that in the context of a plea of contributory negligence it was logically unsupportable to find that a plaintiff was 100 per cent contributorily negligent.

The words "shall be reduced" suggest that where contributory negligence is found there must be some difference between the total loss recorded and the damages awarded. In *McCord* Griffin J., at 165, indicated, however, that in an appropriate case where the fault of the plaintiff was slight as against the fault of the defendant being gross, the plaintiff could be given full damages: see also *JTCN* p.392; *Lavender v. Diamints Ltd* [1949] 1 K.B. 585 and *Hawkins v. Ian Ross (Cashings) Ltd* [1970] 1 All E.R. 180. The court cannot of its own motion reduce the plaintiff's damages: the defence of contributory negligence must be pleaded: *Fookes v. Slaytor* (1978] 1 W.L.R. 1293.

Proviso (a) in subsection (1) is taken from Article 4 of the Convention of Brussels 1910 and section 1 of the Maritime Conventions Act 1911.

Proviso (b) was designed to clarify the law of voluntary assumption of risk. The leading case is *O'Hanlon v. Electricity Supply Board* [1969] I.R. 75. The plaintiff, an experienced electrician in the employment of the defendants, needed a fuse-extractor to carry out in the normal way, and without danger to himself, a particular task given to him by the defendant. Having failed to obtain the fuse-extractor, he could have refused to proceed further with his task or he could have removed fuses from a nearby supply point which would have disconnected the electric current from several houses including the one in which he was working.

The plaintiff, however, proceeded with his task although he knew that he would have to work in close proximity to an un-insulated power line, something he was forbidden to do. The plaintiff received an electric shock and suffered personal injuries. He claimed damages from the defendant's negligence and the defendant denied negligence and pleaded that the plaintiff, well knowing the risk of sustaining injury, voluntarily undertook that risk. In an action in the High Court before Butler J., the jury found that the defendant had been negligent but that the plaintiff had undertaken with full knowledge and voluntarily the risk of injury involved in his conduct. Judgment was therefore entered for the defendant. On appeal, the Supreme Court by a majority (Haugh J. dissenting) ordered a re-trial. Walsh J. (Ó Dálaigh C.J., Budd and Fitzgerald JJ. concurring) said, at 90, that what used to be called the defence of *volenti non fit injuria* was now more properly to be described as the statutory defence that the plaintiff before the act complained of agreed to waive his legal rights in respect of it. In his opinion, the use of the word 'agreed' "necessarily contemplates some sort of intercourse or communication between the plaintiff and defendants from which it could be reasonably inferred that the plaintiff had assured the defendants that he waived any right of action that he might have in respect of the negligence of the defendants." He continued at 92:

> A one-sided secret determination on the part of the plaintiff to give up his right of action for negligence would not amount to an agreement to do so. Such a determination or consent may be regarded as 'voluntary assumption of risk' in the terms of the Act but, by virtue of the provisions of the Act and for the purpose of the Act, this would be contributory negligence and not the absolute defence mentioned in the first part of subsection 1(b) of section 34.

Similarly in *Ryan v. Ireland* [1989] I.L.R.M. 544 at 549, Finlay C.J. (Hamilton P., Walsh, Griffin and Hederman JJ. concurring) said that, while it was correct to say that by enlisting in the Irish Army and by subsequently volunteering for United Nations service in the Lebanon the plaintiff accepted the risks inherent in the possibility of being involved in armed conflict, it could not be implied that he accepted the risk of being unnecessarily exposed to injury by negligence.

To appreciate the change wrought by the provision contrast *McComiskey v. McDermott* [1974] I.R. 75 with *Bennett v. Tugwell* [1971] 2 Q.B. 267 on the effect of notices attached to a car's dashboard to the effect that 'passengers travel at their own risk'. For a case where it was found that the plaintiff had agreed to absolve the defendants from liability: see *Regan v. Irish Automobile Club Ltd* [1990] 1 I.R. 278.

The distinction between the absolute statutory defence and that of contributory negligence is well illustrated by the decision of the Supreme Court in *Judge v. Reap* [1968] I.R. 217. The plaintiff voluntarily accepted a lift in the defendant's car at a time when the plaintiff knew or ought to have known that the defendant was drunk. The defendant crashed the car and the plaintiff was injured. The defendant argued that the plaintiff knew of the risk of injury and must therefore be taken to have expressly or impliedly consented to run the said risk. The Supreme Court observed that knowledge of a risk was not in law consent to that risk (see also Bowen L.J. in *Thomas v. Quartermaine* (1887) 18 Q.B.D. 685 at 696, "the maxim is not *scienti non fit injuria* but *volenti*"). The Court said that, while there were no facts on which it could infer a bargain by the plaintiff to give up his right of action for negligence, it was quite clear that if a person knows or should know that a driver is by reason of the consumption of alcohol not fit to drive and who nevertheless goes as the driver's passenger he must be found guilty of contributory negligence.

To similar effect is the decision of the Supreme Court of Canada in *Dube v. Labar* (1986) 27 D.L.R. (4th) 653, where it was held (*per* Estey J.) that the defence would only arise where the circumstances were such that it was clear that the plaintiff, knowing of the virtually certain risk of harm, bargained away his right to sue for injuries incurred as a result of any negligence on the defendant's part. It should be noted that the English courts still adhere to the view that the *volenti* defence applies to situations such as those in *Morris v. Murray* [1991] 2 Q.B. 6 (pet. dis. [1991] 1 W.L.R. 1362) where the plaintiff knowingly and willingly embarked on a flight with a drunken pilot (see Williams (1991) 54 M.L.R. 745).

Under subsection 2(b) negligent or careless failure to mitigate damage is deemed to be contributory negligence in respect of the amount of which such damage exceeds the damage that would otherwise have occurred. This provision ensures that the plaintiff's failure to mitigate will no longer constitute a complete bar to recovery in respect of such additional mitigable damage. The relevant English cases are discussed in White, *Irish Law of Damages* (1989), pp.31–35.

Section 9(2) of the Liability for Defective Products Act 1991 provides that, where any damage is caused partly by a defect in a product and partly by the fault of the injured person or of any person for whom the injured person is responsible, the provisions of the 1961 Act concerning contributory negligence shall have effect "as if the defect were due to the fault of every person liable by virtue of this Act for the damage caused by the defect".

Identifications

35.—(1) For the purpose of determining contributory negligence—

(a) a plaintiff shall be responsible for the acts of a person for whom he is, in the particular circumstances, vicariously liable;

(b) a plaintiff in an action brought for the benefit of the dependants of a deceased person under Part IV (whether such plaintiff is the personal representative or a dependant of the deceased) shall be deemed to be responsible for the acts of the deceased;

(c) a plaintiff suing as personal representative of the person suffering the damage shall be deemed to be responsible for the acts of such person;

(d) a plaintiff suing on behalf of another (in this section called a nominal plaintiff) shall be deemed to be responsible for the acts of that other (in this section called the beneficiary) and, in particular, a person suing as personal representative of a deceased person shall be deemed to be responsible for the acts of those who would profit by success in the action, including the dependants of the deceased where the action is brought under Part IV: provided that—

(i) where a nominal plaintiff is suing on behalf of more than one beneficiary and one beneficiary has been guilty of contributory negligence while another beneficiary has not, the provisions of subsection (1) of section 34 shall apply only in respect of the share of the beneficiary guilty of contributory negligence; and the provisions of section 21 shall apply in favour of the defendant against the beneficiary so guilty of contributory negligence, in respect of the sum payable by the defendant for the benefit of the beneficiary not guilty of contributory negligence;

(ii) where it is found to be more convenient, the court may allow a nominal plaintiff to recover in full notwithstanding the contributory negligence of a beneficiary, and the provisions of section 21 shall then apply in favour of the defendant against the beneficiary so guilty of contributory negligence;

(e) a plaintiff suing as assignee of another, whether by operation of law or otherwise, shall be deemed to be responsible for the acts of that other;

(f) where the plaintiff's damage was caused by two or more persons and such persons would have been concurrent wrongdoers were it not for a contract by the plaintiff with one of such persons before the occurrence of the damage exempting that person from liability, the plaintiff shall be deemed to be responsible for the acts of that person;

(g) where the plaintiff's damage was caused by concurrent wrongdoers and before the occurrence of the damage the liability of one of such wrongdoers was limited by contract with the plaintiff to a sum less than that wrongdoer's just share of liability between himself and the other wrongdoer as determined under section 21 apart from such contract, the plaintiff shall be deemed to be responsible for the acts of that wrongdoer;

(h) where the plaintiff's damage was caused by concurrent wrongdoers and after the occurrence of the damage the liability of one of such wrongdoers is discharged by release or accord made with him by the plaintiff while the liability of the other wrongdoers remains, the plaintiff shall be deemed to be responsible for the acts of the wrongdoer whose liability is so discharged;

(i) where the plaintiff's damage was caused by concurrent wrongdoers and the plaintiffs claim against one wrongdoer has become barred by the Statute of Limitations or any other limitation enactment, the plaintiff shall be deemed to be responsible for the acts of such wrongdoer;

(j) where the plaintiff's damage was caused by concurrent wrongdoers and, in an action against one of such wrongdoers, judgment is given for the defendant and the plaintiff then brings an action against another of such wrongdoers, the plaintiff shall be deemed to be responsible for the acts of the successful defendant if the defendant now sued can prove that he and the successful defendant were in fact concurrent wrongdoers;

(k) a plaintiff who is responsible for the acts of another under paragraphs (a) to (j) of this subsection shall be responsible also for the acts of any other persons for whose acts the said other person would be responsible under the said paragraphs if he were plaintiff in the action.

(2) For the purpose of subsection (1) of section 34, the contributory negligence—

(a) of a nominal plaintiff; or

(b) (where the action is brought for the loss of the consortium or services of a wife or for the loss of the services of a child or servant) of a wife, child or servant, shall [, subject to paragraph (a) of subsection (1) of this section,] neither bar recovery nor reduce the damages awarded; but the provisions of section 21 shall apply in favour of the defendant against the said nominal plaintiff, wife, child or servant, as the case may be.

(3) Nothing in subsection (1) of this section shall affect the rights of the plaintiff against, or render the plaintiff liable in damages for the acts of a person for whose acts he is deemed by the said subsection to be responsible.

(4) Where a plaintiff is held to be responsible for the acts of another under this section and his damages are accordingly reduced under subsection (1) of section 34, the defendant shall not be entitled to contribution under section 21 from the person for whose acts the. plaintiff is responsible.

GENERAL NOTE

The words in square brackets in subsection (2) were inserted by section 4 of the Civil Liability (Amendment) Act 1964.

For the purpose of determining contributory negligence, eleven cases of identification of the plaintiff are provided for in subsection (1). In general the existing law was put into statutory form. It was the view of the English Law Commission, however, that paragraphs (g), (h), (i) and (j) of subsection (1) improved the contribution rights of a defendant at the expense of the plaintiff: see Working Paper No. 59, *Contribution* (1975) at p.7.

The provisions of subsection 2(b) were considered by the Supreme Court in *McKinley v. Minister for Defence* [1992] 2 I.R. 333. The minority (Finlay C.J. and Egan J.) thought that the subsection was constitutionally infirm but McCarthy J., and by implication Hederman J., refused to entertain the Attorney General's argument challenging the constitutionality of the subsection. O'Flaherty J., who agreed with Hederman and McCarthy JJ. that the action *per quod consortium amisit* extended to a wife, said that the subsection recognised the existence of the cause of action. Consequently, in an action for loss of consortium, whether brought by a husband or a wife, the damages will not be reduced by reason of the injured spouse's contributory negligence: see *Coppinger v. Waterford County Council* [1996] 2 I.L.R.M. 427.

Set-off of claims

36.—(1) When judgment is given for the plaintiff on a claim and for the defendant on a counterclaim under subsection (1) of section 34, the one judgment shall be set off against the other and only the balance found owing shall be recoverable.

(2) This section shall apply notwithstanding that one party is a bankrupt or (where a personal representative is party to an action) that the estate administered by him is insolvent.

(3) This section, and also [paragraph 17(1) of the First Schedule to the Bankruptcy Act 1988], in so far as it applies to a set-off of judgment debts owing by and to a bankrupt, shall operate only in relation to the satisfaction of debts, and, for all purposes (including the construction of policies of insurance) other than that aforesaid, a judgment shall be treated as creating a debt, duty, obligation and liability for the full amount of the judgment as if there were no set-off and for such other purposes a debt (whether by judgment or otherwise) shall be deemed to be paid by the judgment debtor to the extent of a debt set off against it.

(4) Notwithstanding anything in section 62 where a claim is made against a

person who is insured in respect of a liability alleged in that claim and the claim is paid by the insurer with a deduction in respect of a sum owed to the insured by the person making such claim, the insured or any person representing or deriving title under him shall be entitled to recover from the insurers the amount of the said deduction.

[(5) Notwithstanding anything in section 62 where a claim is made against a person who is insured in respect of a liability alleged in that claim and the claim is not paid by the insurer by reason of its being set off in full against a sum owed to the insured by the person making such claim, the insured or any person representing or deriving title under him shall be entitled to recover from the insurers the amount of such claim.]

GENERAL NOTE

The words in square brackets in subsection (3) were substituted by virtue of paragraph 17(2) of the First Schedule to the Bankruptcy Act 1988. Subsection (5) was added by virtue of section 5 of the Civil Liability (Amendment) Act 1964.

The section deals with the set-off of claims. Note that the Rules of the Superior Courts 1986, Ord. 21, r. 16 provide:

> Where in any action a set-off or counterclaim is established as a defence against the plaintiff's claim, the Court may, if the balance is in favour of the defendant, give judgment for the defendant for such balance, or may otherwise adjudge to the defendant such relief as he may be entitled to upon the merits of the case.

Subsection (2) provides that the section shall apply "notwithstanding that one party is a bankrupt" and the Bankruptcy Act 1988 continues this provision: see First Schedule, paragraph 17(2).

Estoppel in case of contributory negligence

37.—(1) Where a plaintiff has his damages reduced under subsection (1) of section 34 on account of contributory negligence and the defendant subsequently brings an action against the plaintiff in respect of damage arising out of the same facts, the determination of liability and the apportionment of fault in the first action shall be binding between the parties in the second action.

(2) Subsection (1) of this section shall apply between two parties notwithstanding that one of them is party to the two actions in different capacities.

GENERAL NOTE

This section applies the doctrine of *res judicata* to findings on the issue of apportionment of fault. Where a plaintiff has his or her damages reduced under section 34 on account of contributory negligence, a defendant who subsequently brings an action, against the plaintiff in respect of damage arising out of the same facts will be bound by the determination of liability and the apportionment of responsibility in the first action. Although the section is designed to encourage the defendant to establish his or her rights by counterclaim in the first action, this may not be possible where there is a large disparity between the claims. There is no requirement that the first action have been heard in a court of co-ordinate or superior jurisdiction. So where A and B are involved in a road traffic accident, with A sustaining minor damage to his motor vehicle and B suffering serious personal injuries, and A sues B in the District Court for the damage to the car, the District Judge's decision will conclude the question of the apportionment of fault in any subsequent High Court proceedings brought by B against A.

In *Donohue v. Brown* [1986] I.R. 90, the plaintiff commenced High Court proceedings claiming damages for personal injuries against the owner and the driver of a motor vehicle which had collided with the plaintiff. The first defendant (the car's owner) had earlier brought District Court proceedings against the plaintiff claiming damages for the damage to her car and, on appeal to the Circuit Court, succeeded, the judge holding that sole responsibility for the damage claimed rested with the plaintiff. In the High Court, Gannon J. held that the plaintiff's action failed against both defendants as the issue of responsibility for the accident had been determined against the plaintiff in the Circuit Court not only as between the plaintiff and the first defendant, but also as between the plaintiff and the second defendant (who had not been a party to the earlier proceedings). Admittedly the circumstances were special in that the first defendant was sued as being vicariously liable for the second defendant's negligence so that there was a complete identity of interest as between the two defendants but White (*op. cit.*, p.72), is critical of the decision in principle on the ground that it risks serious injustice being done to a person in the position of the second defendant:

> As an estoppel by *res judicata* must be mutual, it follows that the second defendant was equally bound by the findings of the Circuit Court as regards responsibility for the accident. Had the Circuit Court, therefore, found in favour of the plaintiff and had the second defendant sustained injuries in the accident, he would have been precluded from bringing a subsequent action against the plaintiff in respect of such injuries although not a party to the proceedings grounding the estoppel.

Subsequently, however, Gannon J.'s decision in *Donohue* was distinguished by Johnson J. in *Reamsbottom v. Raftery* [1991] 1 I.R. 531. Here the plaintiff had brought an action in the High Court against the defendant claiming damages for personal injuries arising out of a road traffic accident. In the accident, a car driven by the plaintiff and owned by her husband collided with a car owned and driven by the defendant. Previously, the defendant had sued the plaintiff's husband in the Circuit Court and the then President of the Circuit Court, Judge O'Malley, had found 100 per cent in favour of the defendant in the High Court action. The plaintiff in the High Court action had not been a party to the Circuit Court action, was not represented therein and did not give evidence but the defendant sought to have her case dismissed on the ground that the same was *res judicata*. Johnson J. observed that it had been open to the defendant to have made the plaintiff a party to the Circuit Court action, and to the plaintiff's husband to have made her a third-party, but that neither of these courses had been pursued. Consequently, if the defendant was correct the situation would arise where the plaintiff was precluded from bringing her case to court because of the result of an action to which she was not a party and over which she had no control. Johnson J. said that an injustice could quite clearly be done if the plaintiff had wished to give evidence or was dissatisfied with the manner in which the Circuit Court case was conducted or wanted to call evidence which was not called before. Since no privity existed between the plaintiff and her husband, the defendant could not prevent her from making a claim by relying on the decision of a case to which she was not a party.

The issue ultimately came before the Supreme Court in *Lawless v. Bus Éireann* [1994] 1 I.R. 474. The plaintiff was the widow of HL who had been killed as a result of a collision between his motor vehicle and the defendant's bus. A passenger in the bus sued Bus Éireann and a nominee of HL's insurance company (representation not having been raised to his estate) and Judge Smith in the Circuit Court held that both HL and Bus Éireann had been negligent and apportioned liability 70 per cent against HL and 30 per cent against Bus Éireann. On Bus Éireann's appeal to the High Court it was decided by Barr J. that the appeal should be allowed and that judgment should be entered solely against the insurance company's nominee.

By way of defence to the plaintiff's action against Bus Éireann, it was pleaded that she was estopped from prosecuting and maintaining the proceedings upon the grounds that the same were *res judicata*, the issue of liability having been determined before Barr J. In an unreported judgment delivered on March 25, 1992, Johnson J. followed his reasoning and the authorities he had relied on in his previous decision in *Reamsbottom*, ruling that the plea of *res judicata* was not sustained. On appeal to the Supreme Court, O'Flaherty J. (with whom Finlay C.J. and Denham J. concurred) followed Johnson J.'s reasoning "in all respects" and adopted the authorities relied on (including the decision of the Northern Ireland

Court of Appeal in *Shaw v. Sloan* [1982] N.I. 393) by the learned High Court judge. O'Flaherty J. pointed out that neither the plaintiff, her children nor HL's other statutory dependants had been represented in any sense at the earlier hearings before Judge Smith and, on appeal, before Barr J. In his view it was "impossible to conclude" that there was any "privity of interest" between the insurance company's nominee and the plaintiff and the deceased's dependants. Their interests were not identical.

Lawless was distinguished by Judge Sheridan in *Holmes v. Dursley Ltd* [1997] *Irish Law Log Weekly*, No. 28/97, October 16, 1997, p. 311. The plaintiff suffered personal injuries following a collision between the car in which she was travelling and a car owned by the first-named defendant and driven by the second-named defendant. The plaintiff's husband instituted proceedings in the District Court against the first-named defendant only and in those proceedings the first-named defendant applied to join the third-party. When the matter came on for hearing, the learned District Court judge found for the plaintiff's husband and apportioned liability 20 per cent against the first-named defendant and 80 per cent against the third-party. The plaintiff then instituted proceedings in the Circuit Court and the issue arose as to whether the parties were bound by the decision of the District Court as to the apportionment of liability, the matter being *res judicata*. It was submitted on behalf of the third-party that it was not estopped from raising the issue of liability because the possible liability of the second-named defendant had not been considered by the District Court. The second-named defendant (the driver) was not, the third-party submitted, a privy to the first-named defendant (the owner) and, accordingly, his liability still fell to be considered. Judge Sheridan, however, took the view that, unlike *Lawless*, the first and second-named defendants enjoyed joint representation and made no distinction in their respective defences as to the relationship between the owner and the driver of the vehicle. Judge Sheridan also said that it was clear that the second-named defendant considered himself bound by the decision in the District Court proceedings, irrespective of the issue of privity of interest between himself and the first-named defendant. In these circumstances, Judge Sheridan was satisfied that the third-party was estopped from revisiting the issue of liability.

A slightly different issue arose in *McCauley v. McDermot* [1997] 2 I.L.R.M. 486. Here a collision had occurred between a car and a tractor. The plaintiff was a passenger in the car, which was owned by her father and driven by the third-party. The tractor was owned but not driven by the defendant. As a result of the impact between the car and the tractor there was a further collision between the tractor and a car owned by DF. The plaintiff's father instituted proceedings in the District Court against the tractor owner claiming damages in respect of the damage to his car. The District Court judge found that both drivers had been negligent and liability was apportioned equally. On appeal, Judge Sheehy found that the accident was due to the negligence of the tractor driver and that there was no contributory negligence on the part of the car driver (the third-party in the present proceedings). DF then instituted proceedings in respect of the damage to her car against the car owner (the plaintiff's father), the car driver, the tractor driver (the defendant in the present proceedings) and the tractor owner. Notice of discontinuance was subsequently served on the car owner and the car driver and DF's claim against the tractor owner and tractor driver was ultimately settled.

The present proceedings were instituted on behalf of the plaintiff against the tractor owner claiming damages in respect of injuries allegedly sustained by her in the collision with the tractor. The tractor owner then sought and was granted liberty to issue and serve a third-party notice against the car driver claiming contribution and indemnity. The car driver then sought (pursuant to the Rules of the Superior Courts 1986, Ord. 16, r. 7) to have the third-party notice set aside on the grounds that the issues arising between him and the tractor owner were *res judicata* or, alternatively, that the third-party proceedings constituted an abuse of the process of the court. The application was dismissed by Murphy J. but, on appeal, the Supreme Court (Hamilton C.J., Barrington and Keane JJ.), in a unanimous judgment delivered by Keane J., set aside the third-party notice.

Keane J. held that, although the car driver was not the privy of the plaintiff's father (the car owner) and, accordingly, there was no ground for invoking the doctrine of issue estoppel, the tractor owner was seeking to relitigate an issue which was conclusively and finally determined against him in the Circuit Court proceedings. The Supreme Court, in these circumstances, felt that this was a clear case of an abuse of process and on that ground set aside the order of the High Court granting liberty to issue the third-party notice.

When proceedings are pending in the District or Circuit Court the mere fact that related proceedings are pending in the High Court is not of itself sufficient to entitle the defendant to the action in the lower court to an adjournment of the action in that court until the determination of the High Court proceedings. This was made clear by McWilliam J. in *Murphy v. Hennessy* [1984] I.R. 378. He concluded that the legislature's intention, with section 37, where two actions between the same parties were commenced, one in the High Court and one in the Circuit Court, the first action would determine the degree of fault in the second action-whichever action came to hearing first. It would appear, however, from Barr J.'s decision in *Gay O'Driscoll Ltd. v. Kotsonouris*, unreported, High Court, December 15, 1986, that an adjournment of the proceedings in the lower court may be granted where the defendant in those proceedings pays into court the sum claimed by the plaintiff in that action.

Liability of concurrent wrongdoers where plaintiff guilty of contributory negligence

38.—(1) Where an action is brought against one or more of concurrent wrongdoers by an injured person who is found in such action to have been guilty of contributory negligence and it is held to be just and equitable that the plaintiff's damages should be reduced under subsection (1) of section 34 having regard to his contributory negligence the judgment against one wrongdoer shall not be for the whole of the plaintiff's recoverable damages but the court shall determine the respective degrees of fault of the plaintiff and of all the defendants to the plaintiff's claim at the time of judgment, leaving out of account the degrees of fault of persons who are not such defendants, and shall give the plaintiff a several judgment against each defendant for such apportioned part of his total damages as the court thinks just and equitable having regard to that defendant's degree of fault determined as aforesaid.

(2) The plaintiff, at any time within the period limited by law for the enforcement of judgments and upon proof that, after taking reasonable steps, he has failed to obtain satisfaction of any judgment in whole or in part, shall have liberty to apply for secondary judgment having the effect of distributing the deficiency among the other defendants in such proportions as may be just and equitable.

(3) This section shall not apply where one of the defendant wrongdoers is responsible for the acts of another; such wrongdoers shall, subject to subsection (1) of section 34, be liable to the plaintiff for a single portion of his damages.

(4) After judgment has been given in accordance with subsection (1) of this section, the plaintiff shall not be entitled to bring a second or subsequent action against a concurrent wrongdoer against whom judgment has not been given, unless he satisfies the court in such action that it was not reasonably possible for him to join such wrongdoer as co-defendant in the first action.

(5) The plaintiff when commencing such second or subsequent action, shall be under a duty to the wrongdoers already successfully sued who have a right of contribution against the wrongdoer now sued or proposed to be sued to take reasonable steps to notify them of such second or subsequent action at least fourteen days before the institution of proceedings in such action or as soon as is reasonably possible after the commencement of such period.

(6) A wrongdoer receiving such notice shall have the right to become co-plaintiff in the action if the proceedings have not been instituted and otherwise to apply to the court for leave to be joined as co-plaintiff or for consolidation of actions; and a wrongdoer who unreasonably fails to take any of those steps as aforesaid shall be barred from his right of contribution.

(7) If the plaintiff is successful in such second or subsequent action, he shall be entitled to the difference between the total of the damages awarded to him in the previous judgment or judgments and the total of damages that in the view of the court would have been awarded if the said wrongdoer had been joined with the previous defendant or defendants as co-defendant in the earlier action or actions; and he shall be entitled in addition to the provision mentioned in subsection (2) of this section: provided that—

(a) nothing in this subsection shall entitle a plaintiff to recover from such wrongdoer more than he could have recovered had he not brought such previous action or actions;

(b) nothing in this subsection shall preclude such wrongdoer from disputing any issue that he is otherwise entitled to dispute and, if the plaintiff's damages are found to be less than they were held to be by the court in the earlier action or actions, such wrongdoer shall not be liable for more than his due proportion as between himself, the plaintiff and the previous defendant or defendants of the damages so found;

(c) such wrongdoer may at his option avail himself of any matter decided against the plaintiff in such previous action or actions as though such matter were *res judicata* between them.

(8) Where damages are awarded against a wrongdoer in accordance with the provisions of this section, such wrongdoer may recover contribution from any other wrongdoer not sued at the same time where such recovery is just and equitable subject to the provisions of Chapter II of this Part.

(9) A wrongdoer, when commencing such action for contribution, shall be under a duty to the injured person who has a right of action against the contributor and to the other wrongdoers already successfully sued by the injured person who have a right of contribution against the contributor to take reasonable steps to notify them of such action for contribution at least fourteen days before the institution of proceedings in such action or as soon as is reasonably possible after the commencement of such period.

(10)The injured person or a wrongdoer receiving such notice shall have the rights specified in subsection (6) of this section, and if he unreasonably fails to take advantage of his rights he shall be barred from his right of action for damages or for contribution as the case may be.

(11) Where the injured person brings a second or subsequent action in accordance with the provisions of this section, and where a wrongdoer brings an action for contribution as provided in subsection (8) of this section, the parties to the action shall be bound by the apportionment of fault made in the earlier actions or actions: but the defendant shall not be bound by such apportionment of provision comes to be made for distributing any deficiency caused by the failure to obtain satisfaction of any judgment in whole or in part from one or the wrongdoers already sued.

(12) Where—
   (a) the plaintiff sues one wrongdoer and either because he obtains judgment by default or because the court negatives contributory negligence the plaintiff recovers judgment in respect of the whole of his damages against such wrongdoer, and
   (b) the plaintiff subsequently sues another wrongdoer who is held to have been a concurrent wrongdoer with the first, the plaintiff also being held to have been guilty of contributory negligence as regards both wrongdoers, the defendant secondly sued shall be entitled to credit for the same proportion of the sum received from the defendant first sued as the proportion of the damage adjudged to be borne by the plaintiff as between himself and the defendant secondly sued, and in the event of overpayment shall be entitled to repayment.

GENERAL NOTE

Although subsection (1) requires that a separate judgment has to be given against each defendant for such apportioned part of the total damages as the court thinks just and equitable having regard to that defendant's degree of fault as determined in the action, it does not follow that a separate and several judgment for costs should be given against each defendant. In *Gillespie v. Fitzpatrick* [1970] I.R. 102, the Supreme Court were of the view that, since there was no provision in the Act, either in section 38 or elsewhere, providing for separate and several judgments relating to costs, the old established law and practice in giving a joint judgment for costs against the defendants prevailed.

The subsection prohibits the court from taking into account the fault of a party who is not a defendant in the plaintiff's action. White, *op. cit.* p. 45, gives the following example to illustrate that it will usually be in a negligent plaintiff's interest, where he has been injured by tortfeasors who are several concurrent wrongdoers, to ensure that all of those wrongdoers are defendants in his action:

> Suppose that P has been injured by the negligence of D1 and the negligence of D2. He sues both and each party to the action is held to be equally responsible for his damage. P will recover 66⅔ per cent of his total damages obtaining a judgment for 33⅓ per cent of the same against each defendant. Now had P merely sued D1, and had D1 then by third-party procedure claimed contribution from D2, the result would be that P would recover judgment for only 50 per cent of his total damages from D1; and D1 would recover contribution from D2 amounting to 25 per cent. of P's total damages.

Subsection (3) provides that the section does not apply where one defendant is vicariously liable for another defendant. As White, *op. cit.*, p. 46, puts it:

> The defendant who is vicariously liable for the wrong of another defendant and that other defendant are, subject to section 34(1), liable to the plaintiff for a single portion of his damages.

So, if P sues three concurrent wrongdoers in respect of damage for which D3 is concerned only as D2's employer "then where, P, D1 and D2 are equally to blame, P's damages will be reduced by 33⅓ per cent, and not (as would be the case if D3's vicarious wrong was counted as a separate wrong with that of D2) 25 per cent." In turn, where D1, D2 and D3 are found liable as concurrent wrongdoers with no contributory negligence on P's part and D3 is concerned only as D2's employer and D1 and D2 are equally to blame: "D1 recovers judgment for contribution against D2 and D3 in respect of only 50 per cent of the plaintiff's recoverable damages and not 66⅔ per cent of such damages".

Bankruptcy of one wrongdoer

39.—Where it is made to appear to the court that—

(a) one wrongdoer in whose favour judgment is given is or may become a bankrupt, or

(b) the estate of one wrongdoer for the benefit of which judgment is given is or may be insolvent,

provision shall be made to ensure that such first-mentioned wrongdoer or such estate, as the case may be, shall be deprived of recovery to the extent that the wrongdoer or estate is liable to another party or in the aggregate to other parties as a result of the same accident, occurrence or transaction; and for that purpose judgment in favour of the wrongdoer or for the benefit of the estate shall, where necessary, be attached in whole or in part for the benefit of another party in whose favour judgment is given.

GENERAL NOTE

This section prevents one wrongdoer who is or may become a bankrupt recovering his loss so long as he owes to the other parties damaged in the same accident more than they owe to him.

Special findings

40.—(1) Where damages are awarded to any person by virtue of subsection (1) of section 34, the jury or if there is no jury then the judge or arbitrator shall find and record—

(a) the total damages that would have been awarded if there had not been contributory negligence;

(b) where the plaintiffs damages are reduced under the said subsection, the proportion of such damages that shall not be awarded to the plaintiff and the proportion that shall be payable by the defendant, or the respective proportions that shall be payable by each of the defendants if more than one expressed In each case in percentage of the total fault of the plaintiff and defendant or defendants;

(c) [....]

(2) It shall be the duty of the judge or arbitrator to make the requisite calculations following upon such findings.

GENERAL NOTE

According to the Explanatory Memorandum accompanying the Bill, this section is "in line with the relevant provisions of section 3 of the British Columbia Contributory Negligence Act 1936" and sets out the findings to be made by the judge, jury or arbitrator where contributory negligence is found. Paragraph (c) of subsection (1) was repealed by section 6 of the Civil Liability (Amendment) Act 1964.

Courts of limited jurisdiction

41.—Where an action is brought in a court of limited jurisdiction, the court may award damages up to the limit of its jurisdiction, even though such damages have first been reduced under subsection (1) of section 34 on account of the plaintiff's contributory negligence.

This section allows the Circuit Court or the District Court to award damages up to the limit of the court's jurisdiction (presently £30,000 and £5,000 respectively), notwithstanding that the damages that would have been awarded, had there not been contributory negligence, are not within the court's jurisdiction. Thus an action for damages may be brought in the Circuit Court where the plaintiff's claim is valued at £100,000 but his damages fall to be reduced by 80 per cent on account of his contributory negligence. In other words, the limit of jurisdiction applies not to the total damages which may be assessed by the judge but rather to the damages which may be awarded.

Costs in cases of contributory negligence

42.—As a general principle, but not so as to limit the judge in the exercise of his discretion, where damages are awarded on claim and counterclaim subject in each case to a reduction for contributory negligence under subsection (1) of section 34, costs shall be awarded in the same proportions as damages.

GENERAL NOTE

This section provides that where damages are awarded on a claim and counterclaim, subject in each case to a reduction for contributory negligence, the liability for costs of the parties, unless the judge otherwise directs, shall be in the same proportion as the liability to make good the loss or damage. The Explanatory Memorandum accompanying the Bill stated that this section followed the legislation in the Canadian provinces of British Columbia, New Brunswick, Nova Scotia and Saskatchewan.

The section was considered by Murnaghan J. in *Noone v. Minister for Finance* [1964] I.R. 63, who took the view that the discretion referred to was a new discretion, the exercise of which was not restricted by what is now the Rules of the Superior Courts 1986, Ord. 99, r. 1. Factors which were not present in the case but which would have influenced his decision to exercise the discretion were (i) the pursuit of a claim contained in a counterclaim mainly to achieve a reduction in the plaintiff's costs and (ii) the awarding of amounts on the claim and counterclaim which were so greatly out of proportion one to the other so as to make the counterclaim unreal in the circumstances.

CHAPTER IV

General

Application for breaches of strict duty

43.—In determining the amount of contribution or of reduction of damages under subsection (1) of section 34 for contributory negligence the court may take account of the fact that the negligence or wrong of one person consisted only in a breach of strict statutory or common-law duty without fault, and may accordingly hold that it is not just and equitable to cast any part of the damage upon such person.

GENERAL NOTE

This section allows the court to take account of the fact that one party is guilty of a breach of strict duty without any negligence and, therefore, to hold that it is not just and equitable to place any responsibility upon that party. The section was considered by Walsh J. in *O'Sullivan v. Dwyer* [1971] I.R. 275, but the learned judge's analysis appears flawed (see White, *op. cit.*, p. 43) since it proceeds on the basis that "where the defendant's wrong is the breach of strict statutory or common law duty without fault there shall be no apportionment of fault as against him", whereas as White points out (*op. cit.*, p. 42) "the section is not mandatory but discretionary". In *Daly v. Avonmore Creameries Ltd* [1984] I.R. 131 at 148, McCarthy J. also expressed difficulty in understanding Walsh J.'s interpretation of section 43 since to him the section appeared to permit but not to compel "absolution from fault" where the defendant's wrong was a breach of a strict statutory or common law duty without fault.

It has been judicially observed (*per* Barron J. in *Dunne v. Honeywell Control Systems Ltd* [1991] I.L.R.M. 595 at 602) that contributory negligence in an action for breach of statutory duty has a different meaning from contributory negligence in an action for negligence at common law. Citing Ó Dálaigh C.J. in *Kennedy v. East Cork Foods Ltd* [1973] I.R. 244, Barron J. said that, in the former case, an employee was not guilty of contributory negligence merely because he was careless or inattentive, or forgetful, or inadvertent. In *Dunne*, the plaintiff sustained injuries when he fell from a ladder on the second-named defendant's premises where, in the course of his employment with the first-named defendant, he was engaged on a repair job. Expert evidence indicated that the ladder did not comply with accepted standards of safety and other evidence showed that the plaintiff had carried a case of tools, provided by the first-named defendant, when ascending and descending the ladder. Barron J. found that both defendants contributed to the accident and apportioned liability as to 80 per cent against the second-named defendant and 20 per cent against the first-named defendant. Both defendants had alleged contributory negligence against the plaintiff and Barron J. was of the view that the plaintiff could not be totally exonerated, in that he had not been taking sufficient care for his own safety, and he would have assessed the degree of fault at common law as being 10 per cent. Having regard, however, to the above mentioned principle of law, the plaintiff was held to be not guilty of contributory negligence in relation to his claim for breach of statutory duty.

One-sided periods of limitation

44.—Where, in any claim for contribution between wrongdoers, or in any case to which subsection (1) of section 34 applies, the defendant avoids liability to the plaintiff by pleading the Statute of Limitations or any other limitation enactment, neither he nor any other person responsible for his acts shall be entitled to recover any damages or contribution from the plaintiff.

GENERAL NOTE

This section, according to the Explanatory Memorandum accompanying the Bill, "is designed to avoid unfairness resulting from any one-sided working of statutes of limitation." The use of the word "shall" indicates that the disentitlement is mandatory.

Restitution

45.—(1) Where, in cases falling within sections 16 or 17 or within subsection (1) of section 35, the defendant owing to ignorance of the facts omits to claim the benefit of the provisions therein contained, the defendant, notwithstanding that judgment has been given in the plaintiff's favour, shall have a right to repayment by the plaintiff of such sum as the plaintiff should not have recovered in virtue of the said provisions.

(2) Where, as a result of the failure to obtain satisfaction of any judgment in whole or in part from one wrongdoer, other concurrent wrongdoers are compelled to bear a larger part of the plaintiff's damage than they would otherwise have borne, or are compelled to pay a larger sum by way of contribution than they would otherwise have paid, they shall have a right of recoupment against such wrongdoer to the extent of the difference.

GENERAL NOTE

This section provides for restitution; specifically that, in the cases provided for, a defendant who, owing to ignorance of the facts, omits to claim the benefits of the relevant provisions of those sections shall, nevertheless, be entitled to repayment by the plaintiff even though judgment has been given in the plaintiff's favour.

Maritime cases

46.—(1)(a) Where, by the fault of two or more vessels, damage is caused to one or more of those vessels or to another vessel or to the cargo of any of those vessels or any property on board, and an action is brought for such damage, the liability of each vessel in respect of such damage shall be in proportion to the degree in which such vessel was in fault and accordingly there shall be no right of contribution in respect of such apportioned liability: provided that—

    (i) if having regard to all the circumstances of the case, it is not possible to establish different degrees of fault, the liability shall be apportioned equally among the vessels in fault;

    (ii) nothing in this subsection shall affect the liability of any person under a contract of carriage or any contract, or shall be construed as imposing any liability upon any person from which he is exempted by any contract or by any provision of law, or as affecting the right of any person to limit his liability in the manner provided by law.

  (b) For the purposes of paragraph (a) of this subsection the liability of a vessel for damage shall mean the liability of those responsible for the proper navigation and management of the vessel.

  (c) Paragraph (a) of this subsection shall not apply to a claim for loss of life or personal injuries.

(2) Where, by the sole or concurrent fault of a vessel damage is caused to that or another vessel or to the cargo or any property on board either vessel, or loss of life or personal injury is suffered by any person on board either vessel, then, subject to subsection (3) of this section, no action shall be maintainable to enforce a claim for damages or lien in respect of such damage, loss of life or injury unless proceedings are commenced within two years from the date when such damage, loss of life or injury was caused; and an action shall not be maintainable to enforce any claim for contribution in respect of an overpaid proportion of any damages for loss of life or personal injuries unless proceedings are commenced within one year from the date of payment.

(3) Any court having jurisdiction to deal with an action to which subsection (2) of this section relates may, subject to any rules of court, extend the period referred to in that subsection to such extent and subject to such conditions as it thinks fit, and shall, if satisfied that there has not during such period been any reasonable opportunity of arresting the defendant vessel within the jurisdiction of the court or within the territorial waters of the country to which the plaintiff's vessel belongs or in which the plaintiff resides or has his principal place of business, extend any such period to an extent sufficient to give such reasonable opportunity.

(4) For the purposes of subsections (1) and (2) of this section, references to

damage caused by the fault of a vessel shall be construed as including references to any salvage or other expenses, consequent upon that fault, recoverable at law by way of damages and such expenses shall be deemed to be a damage caused when they are incurred.

(5) The provisions of this section shall be applied in all cases heard and determined in any court having jurisdiction to deal with the case and in whatever waters the damage in question was caused or the salvage services or other expenses in question were rendered or incurred.

(6) This section shall be construed as one with the Merchant Shipping Acts 1894 to 1952.

GENERAL NOTE

This section provides for maritime cases and subsections (1) and (4) re-enact with amendments section 1 of the Maritime Conventions Act 1911.

The provisions of subsections (2) and (3) have been considered by Barr J. in *Carleton v. O'Regan*, unreported, High Court, October 14, 1996 and *Lawless v. Dublin Port and Docks Board* [1998] 1 I.L.R.M. 514. In the former case, Barr J. was satisfied that the principles laid down in three English cases (*The "Gaz Fountain"* [1987] 2 Lloyd's Rep. 151; *The "Albany"* [1983] 2 Lloyd's Rep. 185, and *The "Al Tabith"* [1993] 2 Lloyd's Rep. 214) as to the basis on which the court should exercise its discretion to extend time for initiating a maritime action in negligence were well founded and were "respectfully" adopted by him. These principles were that time should not to be extended unless the plaintiff could show "special circumstances" and factors which were to be taken into account included the degree of blameworthiness, the length of delay and whether the circumstances which caused the delay were beyond the control of the party who had been dilatory. In the latter case the learned judge confirmed that the section applied to all forms of action in negligence and was not limited to claims made *in rem*. Unlike the former case, Barr J. was satisfied that the plaintiff's explanation for delay was reasonable. It was clearly of some significance, however, that the plaintiff's claim was one for personal injuries and Barr J. expressed concern as to the constitutionality of the section if a plaintiff was disadvantaged by reason of the shorter limitation period merely because of the location of the place of injury, *viz.* on board the vessel.

PART IV

FATAL INJURIES

Definitions (Part IV)

47.—(1) In this Part—

[(1) In this Part—

'dependant' means, in respect of a deceased person whose death is caused by a wrongful act—

    (a) a spouse, parent, grandparent, step-parent, child, grandchild, step-child, brother, sister, half-brother or half-sister of the deceased.

    (b) a person whose marriage to the deceased has been dissolved by a decree of divorce that was granted under the Family Law (Divorce) Act 1996 or under the law of a country or jurisdiction other than the State and is recognised in the State, or

    (c) a person who was not married to the deceased but who, until the date of the deceased's death, had been living with the deceased as husband or wife for a continuous period of not less than three years,

who has suffered injury or mental distress as a result of the death;
'wrongful act' includes a crime.]

(2) In deducing any relationship for the purposes of this Part—

    (a) a person adopted under the Adoption Act 1952 shall be considered the legitimate offspring of the adopter or adopters;

    (b) subject to paragraph (a) of this subsection, an illegitimate person shall be considered the legitimate, offspring off his mother and reputed father;

    (c) a person in *loco parentis* to another shall be considered the parent of that other.

GENERAL NOTE

The words "injury or mental distress" in subsection (1) were considered by the Supreme Court in *McCarthy v. Walsh* [1965] I.R. 246. It was argued that the word "or" was to be read conjunctively so that recovery was only possible where the claimant had sustained both injury and mental distress. The Court, however, held that the word was to be given its ordinary disjunctive meaning and allowed recovery to dependants of the deceased who had only suffered mental distress resulting from the deceased's death.

Subsection (1) was substituted by virtue of section 1 of the Civil Liability (Amendment) Act 1996. The right of action originally conferred by Part IV of the 1961 Act was confined to immediate members of the family and did not extend to cohabitants (see O'Hanlon J. in *Hollywood v. Cork Harbour Commissioners* [1992] 1 I.R. 457 at 466). The effect of the amendment is to extend the definition of dependant in the 1961 Act to include persons who, not being married to one another, had been living together as husband and wife for at least three years before the date of death. It also broadens the definition to include persons whose marriage has been dissolved. Still precluded from recovery are all relations by affinity, except stepchildren and stepparents; remoter relatives, *e.g.* uncles and aunts; cohabitants who were living as husband and wife but who do not satisfy the three-year rule; cohabitants who are involved in a committed sexual relationship but who do not live as husband and wife (*i.e.* same sex partners); and children who are not the deceased's but lived with the deceased while he or she was engaged in a *de facto* relationship with their parent.

Presumably the three-year rule is intended to restrict recovery to those cohabitants who enjoyed a committed relationship with the deceased which amounted to a marriage in all but form. The arbitrary nature of the qualifying time limit, however, entails the potential for injustice in some circumstances. There may be more reliable indications of the commitment of the relationship in question, *e.g.* where the relationship has produced a child. Similarly, in the light of the nature of many modern social relationships, is there any proper justification for the exclusion of recovery by persons financially dependent on the deceased solely on the basis of their sexual preference? It was the view of the English Law Commission in its Consultation Paper No. 148, *Claims for Wrongful Death* (1997) that the list of dependants in the Fatal Accidents Act 1976 (which is wider than that in section 47(1) even as amended) was too restrictive. The Law Commissioners were of the provisional view that the statutory list should be abolished and be replaced either by a test whereby any individual has a right of recovery who had a reasonable expectation of a non-business benefit from continuation of the deceased's life or by a test whereby any individual has a right of recovery who was or, but for the death, would have been dependent, wholly or partly, on the deceased.

Section 1(2) of the 1996 Amendment Act provides that the amendment of section 47(1) of the 1961 Act shall not have effect in relation to a cause of action that accrued before December 25, 1996.

The expression *in loco parentis*, as used in subsection 2(c), was considered by the Supreme Court in *Waters v. Cruikshank* [1967] I.R. 378. The plaintiff, an uncle of the deceased with whom the deceased had been living, instituted a claim under the Fatal Injuries Act 1956. The defendant, whose negligence had caused the death of the deceased, argued for a narrow definition of the phrase, similar to that which had been accepted by Jessel M.R. in *Bennet v. Bennet* (1879) L.R. 10 Ch. D. 474 at 477, namely the assumption of a clear and definite obligation to provide for the deceased. The Supreme Court, however, rejected the argument that a person could only be *in loco parentis* to a deceased if the deceased had been dependent of financial support on the person claiming.

Action where death caused by wrongful act, neglect or default

48.—(1) Where the death of a person is caused by the wrongful act of another such as would have entitled the party injured, but for his death, to maintain an action and recover damages in respect thereof, the person who would have been so liable shall be liable to an action for damages for the benefit of the dependents of the deceased.

(2) Only one action for damages may be brought against the same person in respect of the death.

(3) The action may be brought by the personal representative of the deceased or, if at the expiration of six months from the death there is no personal representative or no action has been brought by the personal representative, by all or any of the dependants.

(4) The action, by whomsoever brought, shall be for the benefit of all the dependants.

(5) The plaintiff shall furnish the defendant with particulars of the person or persons for whom and on whose behalf the action is brought and of the nature of the claim in respect of which damages are sought to be recovered.

(6) [....]

GENERAL NOTE

Subsection (6) was repealed by section 6(6) of the Statute of Limitations (Amendment) Act 1991. The Rules of the Superior Courts 1986, Ord. 22, r. 13 provide that, in any cause or matter in which damages are claimed under Part IV of the Civil Liability Act 1961, "money paid into Court under this Order shall not be paid out without an order of the Court".

Subsection (1) gives a deceased's dependants a cause of action where the deceased's fatal injuries had been caused by the wrongful act (which includes default or other omission) of another person such as would have entitled the deceased to have successfully sued that person in respect thereof. The dependants can thus only recover on the deceased's cause of action if "the deceased had at the time of his death a right. to maintain an action and recover damages for the act, neglect or default of which they complain", *per* Scrutton L.J. in *Nunan v. Southern Railway Co.* [1924] 1 K.B. 223 at 227. Scrutton L.J. went on to say that if the deceased had lost such a right, such as by failing to make a claim within the relevant limitation period or by reason of a release by accord and satisfaction, so that he could not have brought an action at the time of his death, then neither could his dependants bring an action: see respectively *Williams v. Mersey Docks and Harbour Board* [1905] 1 K.B. 804 and *Read v. Great Eastern Railway Co.* (1868) LR 3 QB 555. As White details (*op. cit.*, pp. 316–318) the position is otherwise in the United States of America: see *Sea-Land Services Inc. v. Gandet* (1974) 414 U.S. 573.

The English approach was adopted by Lavan J. in *Mahon v. Burke* [1991] 2 I.R. 495. The deceased had settled his negligence action against the defendants but died shortly thereafter. His widow then brought an action for the benefit of the deceased's dependants (herself, her son and her four daughters, her father-in-law, the deceased's seven brothers and his three sisters). It was argued on her behalf that, where the death of a person is caused by the wrongful act of another such as would have entitled the deceased to maintain an action, such person should still be liable to a dependant of the deceased notwithstanding a compromise by the deceased of his cause of action. This was not accepted by Lavan J, who held that for a plaintiff to succeed under section 48, it must be proven that there was vested in the deceased a cause of action at the time of his or her death.

It should be noted that a dependant who is *sui juris* may waive his or her claim and that any such waiver should be exhibited in the plaintiff's affidavit.

Section 6(1) of the Statute of Limitations (Amendment) Act 1991 provides that an action under this section shall not be brought after the expiration of three years from:

(a)   the date of death, or

(b)   the "date of knowledge" of the person for whose benefit the action is brought,

whichever is the later. As to what is meant by a person's "date of knowledge" see section 2 of the 1991 Act. On the 1991 Act generally, see Kerr, *The Statute of Limitations (Amendment) Act 1991* (1991 Irish Current Law Statutes Annotated, Round Hall Sweet & Maxwell).

Damages

49.—(1)(a) The damages under section 48 shall be—

(i)   the total of such amounts (if any) as [. . .] the judge [. . .] shall consider proportioned to the injury resulting from the death to each of the dependants, respectively, for whom or on whose behalf the action is brought, and

(ii)   subject to paragraph (b) of this subsection, the total of such amounts (if any) as the judge shall consider reasonable compensation for mental distress resulting from the death to each of such dependants.

(b)   The total of any amounts awarded by virtue of sub-paragraph (ii) of paragraph (a) of this subsection shall not exceed [£20,000].

(c)   Each amount awarded by virtue of paragraph (a) of this subsection shall be indicated separately in the award.

(d)   [...]

[(1A) Where the Minister for [Justice, Equality and Law Reform] is satisfied that the monetary amount for the time being standing specified

(a)   in paragraph (b) of subsection (1), or

(b)   in respect of paragraph (b) of subsection (1), by virtue of an order made under this subsection,

should, having regard to changes in the value of money generally in the State since the monetary amount was so specified, be varied, the Minister may by order specify an amount that the Minister considers is appropriate, and in such case paragraph (b) of subsection (1) shall, in relation to any cause of action that accrues while the order is in effect, have effect as if the amount specified in the order were set out in that paragraph.

(1B) Every order made under subsection (1A) shall be laid before each House of the Oireachtas as soon as practicable after it is made and, if a resolution annulling the order is passed by either House within the next 21 days on which that House has sat after the order is laid before it, the order shall be annulled accordingly, but without prejudice to any cause of action that accrued while the order was in effect.]

(2) In addition, damages may be awarded in respect of funeral and other expenses actually incurred by the deceased, the dependants or the personal representative by reason of the wrongful act.

(3) It shall be sufficient for a defendant, in paying money into court in the action, to pay it in one sum as damages for all the dependants without apportioning it between them.

(4) The amount recovered in the action shall, after deducting the costs not recovered from the defendant, be divided among the persons entitled in such shares as may have been determined.

[(5) Where a person referred to in paragraph (c) of the definition of "dependant" in section 47 (1) had no enforceable right to financial maintenance by the deceased, the court shall take that fact into account, together with any other relevant matter, in determining the damages to be awarded to the person by virtue of subparagraph (i) of paragraph (a) of subsection (1) of this section.]

GENERAL NOTE

The words in square brackets in sub-paragraph (i) of paragraph (a) of subsection (1) were deleted by section 4 of the Courts Act 1988; the figure in square brackets in paragraph (b) of subsection (1) was substituted by section 2(1)(a) of the Civil Liability (Amendment) Act 1996. The words in square brackets in paragraph (d) of subsection (1) were repealed by section 6 of the Civil Liability (Amendment) Act 1964. Subsections (1A) and (1B) were inserted by section 2(1)(b) of the Civil Liability (Amendment) Act 1996. The words in square brackets in subsection (1)(A) were inserted by virtue of the Equality and Law Reform (Transfer of Departmental Administration and Ministerial Functions) Order 1977 (S.I. No. 297 of 1997) and the Justice (Alteration of Name of Department and Title of Minister) Order 1997 (S.I. No. 298 of 1997). Subsection (5) was inserted by section 2(1)(c) of the Civil Liability (Amendment) Act 1996.

The increase in the amount of compensation for mental distress that can be awarded from the previous figure of £7,500 (as provided for by section 28(1) of the Courts Act 1981) does not have effect in relation to a cause of action that accrued before December 25, 1996.

In *Mahon v. Burke* [1991] 2 I.R. 495, Lavan J. said at 500 that subsection (1) provided the machinery for determining the heads or types of damages to which dependants, properly entitled to sue pursuant to section 48, are to be compensated. The damages which may be recovered under paragraph (a)(i) are "in the nature of a compensation for the pecuniary loss sustained by the dependants": *per* Kennedy C.J. in *Gallagher v. Electricity Supply Board* [1933] I.R. 558 at 566. This would include the loss of the money that the deceased brought into the household, the loss of provision of goods and money, and the loss of fringe benefits such as a company car (see *Clay v. Pooler* [1982] 3 All E.R. 570). *Quaere* whether the loss of parent's care, guidance, education, training and affection is a pecuniary loss? See *Vana v. Tosta* (1968) 66 D.L.R. (2d) 97 and *Fisher v. Smithson* (1978) 17 S.A.S.R. 223.

Such loss is not restricted to that which has actually materialised. Prospective loss may also be taken into account. In *Horgan v. Buckley* [1938] I.R. 115 Sullivan C.J. said at 123 that pecuniary loss was established if it was shown that the dependant had a reasonable expectation of pecuniary benefit from the continuance of the life in question and held that it was not a condition precedent to the maintenance of the action that the deceased should have actually been earning money or moneys worth or contributing to the support of the dependant at or before the date of death. Meredith J. at 132 went on to consider the basis of fact upon which a judge is to proceed to estimate loss which for one reason or another might never be incurred and held that the estimate could be made on the basis of a multiple contingency. So, in *O'Sullivan v. Corás Iompair Éireann* [1978] I.R. 409, Griffin J. said at 426 that the value of a dependency could include "not only that part of the earnings of a deceased which he would have expended in maintaining his dependants, but also that part of his earnings which he would have saved and which most likely would have come to his dependants on his death". Similarly, Laffoy J. in *Fitzpatrick v. Furey*, Irish Times Law Reports, August 31, 1998 held that where the dependants had a reasonable prospect of enhancement of pecuniary benefits from the deceased, this was something the Court should take into account in assessing the size of the claim. Laffoy J. also held that public policy precluded her having regard to the deceased's undeclared income in this assessment.

The assessment of the value of the dependency is considered in detail by White, *op. cit.*, pp. 335–357. It must be noted, however, that the dependants' entitlement is to such damages as are "proportioned" to the injury sustained by reason of the death. The word "proportioned" clearly introduces an element of what is reasonable in the circumstances.

The damages awarded should represent the balance of the pecuniary loss, both actual and expected, which the dependants incur in consequence of the deceased's death after deducting any pecuniary gains which accrued to them: see Latham C.J. and Dixon J. in *Public Trustee v. Zoanetti* (1945) 70 C.L.R. 266 at 271 and 276–279 respectively. In this respect the prohibition in section 50 on taking into account pensions or sums payable under an insurance policy must be noted. The benefit derived from the dependants' accelerated succession to the deceased's estate must be taken into account: see, *e.g. Murphy v. Cronin* [1966] I.R. 699 at 710.

It would appear that a deduction may also be made in respect of the possibility of remarriage by a widow or widower dependant (see Barron J. in *Fitzsimons v. Board Telecom Éireann* [1991] 1 I.R. 536 and Barr J. in *Cooper v. Egan*, unreported, High Court, December 20, 1990), since the revival of the capacity to marry is something which the surviving spouse would not have had if the deceased had not died (*Carroll v. Purcell* (1961) 107 C.L.R. 73 at 79). It must be borne in mind, however, that remarriage, if it occurs, may not always terminate the loss of dependency: see Ruttan J. in *Ball v. Kraft* (1966) 60 D.L.R. (2d.) 35 at 42 and Edmund Davies L.J. in *Goodburn v. Thomas Cotton Ltd* [1968] 1 Q.B. 845 at 855–856. The court must therefore adopt a two-stage approach. First, evidence should be directed to establish whether there was a reasonable expectation at the date of the death that this would occur and, secondly, to determine the then value of the benefits accruing to each of the dependants by reason of that remarriage: *per* Barron J. *Fitzsimons v. Board Telecom Éireann* [1991] 1 I.R. 536 at 552. *Quaere* whether similar considerations apply to the adoption of orphaned children?

In *Gallagher v. Electricity Supply Board* [1933] I.R. 558, it was held that the onus rests on the claimant to establish the basis for calculating the loss sustained by the individual dependants on whose behalf the action is brought: on the use of statistical evidence, see *Dowling v. Jedos Ltd*, unreported, Supreme Court, March 30, 1977. Although Kennedy C.J. would appear to have placed the entire burden on the claimant (see [1933] I.R. at 566) the weight of English authority (cited by White, *op. cit.*, p. 327, fn. 18) is to the effect that while the burden of proving gross loss rests with the claimant the burden of proving the deductions to be made from such loss rests with the defendant: see, in particular, *Mead v. Clarke Chapman & Co. Ltd* [1956] 1 W.L.R. 76 at 84.

A controversial issue is the assessment of damages for loss of domestic services. It has long been accepted that the loss of domestic services performed by the deceased is a material loss which may provide a basis for compensation. What is unclear is whether the damages awarded are restricted to the actual past and future monetary loss incurred by replacing the lost services. So, in *Seymour v. British Paints (Australia) Pty Ltd* [1967] Qd. R. 227, the Full Court of the Supreme Court of Queensland (Wanstall and Douglas JJ., Gibbs J. dissenting) held that damages for the loss of such services which would have been rendered by a deceased wife could not be recovered in a fatal injuries action where the evidence failed to show that expense had been incurred or was likely to be incurred by the widower "in employing a servant to keep house for him, or to come by the day and clean and wash and iron, or in having his washing done at a laundry or his meals prepared by a caterer" (*per* Wanstall J. at 228). *Seymour*, however, was not followed in other Australian jurisdictions (see *Naum v. Nominal Defendant* [1974] 2 N.S.W.L.R. 14; *Cornish v. Watson* [1968] W.A.R. 198; *Doody v. Federation Insurance Ltd* (1977) 16 S.A.S.R. 173) and was overruled by the High Court of Australia in *Nguyen v. Nguyen (No. 1)* (1990) 169 C.L.R. 245. Deane J. at 255 said that the fact that financial expenditure was not and will not be incurred in obtaining domestic services did not mean that it was impossible to assess monetary compensation for the need for such service. As McHugh J.A. had put it in *Budget Rent-A-Car Pty Ltd v. Van Der Kemp* [1984] 3 N.S.W.L.R. 303 at 309: "the widower, who does without and fends for himself, suffers loss as much as the widower who replaces the lost services with those of a housekeeper."

This is not to say that dependants are automatically entitled to the benefit of a substantial award of damages in every case where the deceased provided and was likely to provide gratuitous domestic services: see Costello J. in *McDonagh v. McDonagh* [1992] 1 I.R. 119

at 124–125. It must be ascertained whether there was a reasonable need for the services and that question, particularly in the context where the ultimate burden of liability to pay damages will be cast upon the community generally through the cost of insurance premiums, must be answered by reference to current standards and values: per Deane J. in *Nguyen (No. 1)* at 257. So in *McDonagh*, Costello J. said that account must be taken of the fact that services which a mother renders her children is different at different stages of their development. Furthermore account must also be taken of the fact that the services which a mother in full-time employment gives her children must of necessity be less than that given by a mother who works full-time at home: see also Derrington J. in *Nguyen v. Nguyen (No. 2)* [1992] 1 Qd. R. 405 at 412–414. In *Van Gervan v. Fenton* (1992) 175 C.L.R. 327 it was held that, where a plaintiff is entitled to recover damages for the value of services rendered to him gratuitously by his wife, the value of the services is to be assessed, not by reference to what the wife would have earned by remaining in outside employment and has forgone, but by the market value of the services required by the plaintiff.

Likewise, the courts are reluctant to conclude that, where someone, such as a grandparent or an aunt, voluntarily takes over the care of the household, a deduction should be made from the assessment of damages: see *Cooper v. Egan*, unreported, High Court, December 20, 1990 and the English cases of *Rawlinson v. Babcock & Wilcox Ltd* [1967] 1 W.L.R. 481, *Hay v. Hughes* [1975] Q.B. 790; *Spittle v. Bunney* [1988] 1 W.L.R. 847; *Stanley v. Saddique* [1992] 1 Q.B. 1 and *Hayden v. Hayden* [1992] 1 W.L.R. 986. See also the Canadian cases of *Stonehouse v. Gamble* (1983) 44 B.C.L.R. 375; *Plant v. Chadwick* (1986) 5 B.C.L.R. (2d.) 305; *Coe Estate v. Tennant* (1988) 31 B.C.L.R. (2d.) 236; *Whitter v. DeSousa* (1989) 16 A.C.W.S. (3d.) 176 and *Skelding v. Skelding* (1992) 98 D.L.R. (4th) 219. As Barron J. points out, however, in *Fitzsimons v. Bord Telecom Éireann* [1991] 1 I.R. 536 at 552, where voluntary benefits are disregarded it is not because they are voluntary, but because at the date of the death there was no reasonable expectation that they would occur. The Canadian cases, however, proceed on the basis that it would be contrary to public policy to deduct such benefits: see judgment of Cashman J. in *Skelding* at 235.

Damages run from the date of death and are ascertained by reference to facts existing at the date of death. This means that the actual earnings of the deceased are to be ascertained by reference to the date of death and the cost of replacing gratuitously supplied services are to be calculated by reference to costs prevailing at the time of death: *per* Costello J. in *McDonagh v. McDonagh* [1992] 1 I.R. 119 at 123.

Before the enactment of the 1961 Act it was well established that nothing in the nature of a *solatium* for the dependants' injured feelings occasioned by death might lawfully be awarded: see Kennedy C.J. in *Gallagher v. Electricity Supply Board* [1933] I.R. 558 at 566. The reason for this was well put by Jeffrey J. in *Naum v. Nominal Defendant* [1974] 2 N.S.W.L.R. 14 at 16:

> The inexactitude of the statute's language made the judges of a century ago fearful of the liberties a jury might take with the defendant's purse were their deliberations not to be confined by limitations about which the statute itself is quite silent. It was Coleridge J.'s opinion in *Blake v. Midland Railway Co.* (1852) 18 Q.B. 93 at 111, expressed, interestingly enough, in a judgment in which the sponsor of the Act through Parliament [the then Lord Campbell C.J.] concurred that, if it permitted a calculation by the jury other than of the pecuniary loss sustained by members of the family from the death of one of them, "a serious danger might arise of damages being given to the ruin of defendants".

Paragraph (a)(ii) of subsection (1), however, provides a limited remedy for damages in respect of mental distress. The maximum aggregate of the sums awarded under this heading was initially £1,000, but this was increased to £7,500 by the Courts Act 1981 and then to £20,000 by the Civil Liability (Amendment) Act 1996. The award of compensation for mental distress was described by the Minister for Equality and Law Reform as a "statutory acknowledgement" that the pain and grief suffered by those in a "family type relationship" merited "court recognition" when a compensation award was being made (Vol. 469 *Dáil Debates* Col. 1323).

The leading case on the method of assessment of this type of damages is *McCarthy v.*

Walsh [1965] I.R. 246. Here Ó Dálaigh C.J. stressed that the test to be applied was that damages for mental distress were to be reasonable and that the term "reasonable" was not to be equated with "moderate" or "small". In his view, this precluded damages being measured by reference to an "imagined worse case". The statutory limit he said was a limit on what might be recovered. It was not a limit on what was reasonable. So, if reasonable damages for mental distress exceed £20,000 then the figure must be reduced to the statutory maximum and if there are two or more dependants their damages will abate proportionately. See also Walsh J. in *Dowling v. Jedos Ltd*, unreported, Supreme Court, March 30, 1977. On *solatium* generally see Veitch, "Solatium–A Debt Repaid" (1972) 7 Ir. Jur. (N.S.) 77.

Subsection (2), which re-enacts section 4(2) of the Fatal Injuries Act 1956, confers an entitlement to damages "in respect of funeral and other expenses" in favour of a defendant properly entitled to sue pursuant to section 48. The subsection, therefore, cannot be interpreted so as to enable a plaintiff to maintain an action in respect of the deceased's funeral expenses notwithstanding the deceased's settlement of his action: *per* Lavan J. in *Mahon v. Burke* [1991] 2 I.R. 495 at 500. When considering the equivalent provision in the English legislation, the courts have held that, to be recoverable, the funeral expenses must be reasonable in all the circumstances, including the deceased's station in life, creed, and racial origin. The use of the expression "funeral and other expenses" is specifically wider than the equivalent English provision: White, *op. cit.*, p. 419, suggests that "other expenses" need not have been incurred *after* the death. White also suggests, *op. cit.*, pp. 422–423, that expenses typically recoverable include the costs of a grave, coffin, embalming, tombstone, death habit, wreaths, and transportation of the corpse; travelling expenses of dependant mourners; grave diggers', morticians', and undertakers' fees; advertising expenses; the cost of mourning clothes for the dependants; and the cost of a wake. *Quaere* whether the cost of a memorial or monument to the deceased may be recovered?

It should be noted that, at paragraph 9.93 of the Law Reform Commission's *Consultation Paper on Aggravated, Exemplary and Restitutionary Damages* (April 1998), the Commission provisionally recommended that section 49 be amended to allow for the recovery of exemplary damages in wrongful death cases.

No mental distress damages to certain persons

[**49A.**—Notwithstanding anything in this Part, damages may not be awarded to a person referred to in paragraph (b) of the definition of "dependant" in section 47(1) in respect of any mental distress allegedly caused to the person by the death of the deceased.]

GENERAL NOTE

This section, which was inserted by virtue of section 3 of the Civil Liability (Amendment) Act 1996, provides that a divorced spouse will not be entitled to claim damages for mental distress. Section 3(2) of the 1996 Act provides that this section was to come into operation on December 25, 1996.

Sums not to be taken into account in assessing damages

50.—In assessing damages under this Part account shall not be taken of—
  (a) any sum payable on the death of the deceased under any contract of insurance;
  (b) any pension, gratuity or other like benefit payable under statute or otherwise in consequence of the death of the deceased.

GENERAL NOTE

This section re-enacts section 5 of the Fatal Injuries Act 1956 which replaced section 1 of the Fatal Accidents (Damages) Act 1908, which in turn had overturned the rule in *Pym v.*

Great Northern Railway Co. (1863) 4 B. & S. 396. White in *Irish Law of Damages, op. cit.,* p. 360, submits that the rule of non-deduction herein prescribed is "probably only applicable to money payments". He further submits at pp. 362–363 that the phrase "any sum payable on the death of the deceased under any contract of insurance" is merely descriptive of the insurance monies themselves so that "nothing turns upon whether the deceased, and on his death, his estate, has an enforceable right to the monies or upon who the initial payee under the policy is as long as the monies can be identified as the proceeds of insurance when they ultimately reach the hands of the dependants" (citing Pearce L.J. in *Green v. Russell* [1959] 2 Q.B. 226 at 248). Consequently, the deceased need not be a party to the contract of insurance and need not have paid the premium. This conclusion is supported by Geoghegan J.'s decision on the meaning of section 2 of the Civil Liability (Amendment) Act 1964 in *Greene v. Hughes Haulage Ltd* [1997] 3 I.R. 109. Paragraph (a) is in similar terms to section 3(7) of the British Columbian Family Compensation Act 1979, on which see *Knowles Estate v. Walton Estate* (1992) 93 D.L.R. (4th) 734.

In *Murphy v. Cronin* [1966] I.R. 699, the Supreme Court held that, on the death of the deceased before superannuation age, the payment, under the rules of the superannuation fund to which the deceased had been a contributor, of a sum equal to his accumulated contributions with interest to his personal representative and the payment of a sum equal to 25 per cent of such contributions to the widow were both non-deductible. The first sum was "a like benefit" and the second was a "gratuity" within the meaning of paragraph (b).

In *Feeney v. Ging*, unreported, High Court, December 17, 1982, however, Ellis J. held that the section did not render non-deductible sums paid by way of English university grants in respect of the education of the deceased's dependent children.

Social welfare benefits payable to a dependant are not deductible: see *State (Hayes) v. Criminal Injuries Compensation Tribunal* [1982] I.L.R.M. 210 at 212. This proposition is reinforced by section 236(1) of the Social Welfare (Consolidation) Act 1993 which expressly excludes from the assessment of damages any child benefit, survivor's pension, orphan's (contributory) allowance, lone parent's allowance (in the case of a person who qualifies for such allowance by virtue of being a widow or widower) or widow's or orphan's (non-contributory pension). It should be noted, however, that section 75(3) of the 1993 Act provides:

> Notwithstanding section 50 of the Civil Liability Act 1961, in assessing damages in respect of a person's death under Part IV of that Act, account may be taken of any death benefit, by way of grant under section 63 of this Act in respect of funeral expenses, resulting from that person's death.

See also section 2 of the Civil Liability (Amendment) Act 1964 for the sums of which account is not to be taken in cases of personal injury not causing death (page 80 *infra*).

Adaptation of references to Fatal Accidents Acts 1846 to 1908

51.—A reference in any enactment to the Fatal Accidents Acts 1846 to 1908 or to any of them shall be construed as a reference to this Part.

PART V

AMENDMENTS OF THE WORKMEN'S COMPENSATION ACTS 1934 TO 1955

GENERAL NOTE

Sections 52, 53 and 54 amended the Workmen's Compensation Acts 1934 to 1955, but, because those Acts were repealed by the Social Welfare (Occupational Injuries) Act 1966, these sections have been omitted.

Part VI

Amendment of the Air Navigation and Transport Act 1936

55.—*[Substituting a new section for section 18 of the Air Navigation and Transport Act 1936].*

General Note

See now section 4 of the Air Navigation and Transport Act 1965 which substitutes a new section for section 18 (inserted by section 55 of the 1961 Act) of the 1936 Act.

Part VII

Miscellaneous

Abolition of last opportunity rule

56.—For the purposes of subsection (1) of section 34 and subsection (1) of section 46, the fact that any person—

    (a) had an opportunity of avoiding the consequences of the act of any other person but negligently or carelessly failed to do so, or

    (b) might have avoided those consequences by the exercise of care, or

    (c) might have avoided those consequences but for previous negligence or want of care on his part,

shall not, by itself, be a ground for holding that the damage was not caused by the act of such other person.

General Note

This section abolishes the so-called "last opportunity" rule or, as it was sometimes known, the doctrine of "ultimate negligence" or the "last clear chance" rule: on which see MacIntyre, "The Rationale of Last Clear Chance" (1940) 53 Harv. L. Rev. 1225 and MacIntyre, "Last Clear Chance after Thirty Years Under the Apportionment Statutes" (1955) 33 Can. Bar Rev. 257. According to this rule, the plaintiff was entitled to recover, despite his or her own negligence, if the defendant had the last opportunity of avoiding the accident but failed to do so due to negligence: see the discussions in *Alford v. Magee* (1952) 85 C.L.R. 437 at 450–464 and *March v. E & M Stramare Pty Ltd* (1991) 65 A.L.J.R. 334 at 336–338. Although the rule is usually attributed to the decision of Parke B. in *Davies v. Mann* (1842) 10 M. & W. 546, it actually derives from Salmond, writing in the 3rd edition (1912) of his textbook on Torts (see pp. 39–43). In subsequent editions, however, Heuston (see the 20th ed. (1992), pp. 500–502) doubts whether the rule was ever "really law at all, for it seems to have been adopted in no case of good authority in any jurisdiction in the Commonwealth". In any event the rule is unnecessary in a system that allows for contributory negligence (see *JTCN*, p. 223 and *per* Monnin J.A. in *Keough v. Henderson Highway Branch No. 215 of the Royal Canadian Legion* (1978) 91 D.L.R. (3d) 507, 520).

Abolition of defences

57.—(1) It shall not be a defence in an action of tort merely to show that the plaintiff is in breach of the civil or criminal law.

(2) It shall not be a defence in an action for breach of statutory duty merely to show that the defendant delegated the performance of the duty to the plaintiff.

Miscellaneous

Subsection (1) provides that it shall not be a defence merely to show that the plaintiff was in breach of the civil or criminal law. The subsection, however, does not go so far as to abolish the *ex turpi causa* doctrine. As Barwick C.J. said in *Jackson v. Harrison* (1978)138 C.L.R. 438 at 446:

> A defence of illegality that the plaintiff, at the time his cause of action arose, was in breach of statute is, in my opinion, a different field of discourse altogether from a defence that the plaintiff has no cause of action against the defendant because of their joint participation in an illegal activity. Reasoning apt in the former connection is not directly appropriate to the latter.

This latter doctrine has a long history. In *Colburn v. Patmore* (1834) 1 C.M. & R. 73, Lord Lyndhurst C.B. said at 83 that he knew of no case "in which a person who has committed an act declared by the law to be criminal, has been permitted to recover compensation against a person who has acted jointly with him in the commission of the crime."

The leading Irish case is *O'Connor v. McDonnell*, unreported, High Court (1969 No. 1382P), June 30, 1970. The plaintiff, defendant and others had gone off at 0200 hrs on an expedition with the avowed intention of shooting deer on Torc mountain. During this escapade, the defendant shot the plaintiff by mistake. Murnaghan J. had no doubt that the plaintiff and defendant were *participes criminis* and that the courts could not entertain the plaintiff's action as a matter of public policy. The learned judge said that reference to statutes such as the Game Act (Ireland) 1698 and 1787 and the Night Poaching Acts 1828 and 1862 made it obvious that the plaintiff and defendant "were engaged in an unlawful adventure". He was also satisfied that the *dictum* of Lord Mansfield in *Holman v. Johnston* (1775) 1 Cowp. 341, that the courts will not lend their aid to persons who founded their cause of action upon illegal acts "succinctly and clearly" laid down the applicable legal principle which had in no way been affected by section 57(1). See also the dismissal by District Justice Brennan of a claim for damages by the operator of a "pirate" radio station on the ground that the courts could not be used by people pursuing activities which were a flagrant breach of the law: *Hardy v. Caffrey, The Irish Times*, February 11, 1987.

This broadly-based doctrine of illegality has been subjected to rigorous examination by the High Court of Australia on a number of occasions and has given rise to considerable commentary: see, *e.g.* Ford, "Tort and Illegality: The *Ex Turpi Causa* Defence in Negligence Law" (1977–1978) 11 Melbourne Univ. L.R. 32 and 164 and Swanton, "Plaintiff a Wrongdoer: Joint Complicity in an Illegal Enterprise as a Defence to Negligence" (1981) 9 Sydney Law Rev. 309.

The first time the court was given the opportunity to examine the doctrine was in *Smith v. Jenkins* (1970) 119 C.L.R. 397. Here the plaintiff and defendant stole a car together and the plaintiff was seriously injured due to the defendant's careless driving. The plaintiff was unsuccessful in his claim for damages on the ground that the relationship of one participant to another in the commission of an offence was not such as to give rise to a duty of care *inter se* in relation to acts done in the commission of the offence. In the view of the Court (Barwick CJ, Kitto, Windeyer, Owen and Walsh JJ.) the plaintiff and defendant were "adventurers in crime, not neighbours". Windeyer J. observed at 422 that if two people participated in the commission of a crime each accepted the risk of negligence of the other in the actual performance of the criminal act. As Scrutton L.J. pointed out in *Hillen v. I.C.I. (Alkali) Ltd* [1934] 1 K.B. 455, it would be absurd for the judiciary to determine the standard of care appropriate of a prudent criminal:

> A court will not hear evidence nor will it determine a standard of care owing by a safe-blower to his accomplice in respect of the explosive device.

See also *Bondarenko v. Sommers* (1968) 69 S.R. (N.S.W.) 269. But what of acts committed prior or subsequent to the criminal offence? The principle laid down by the High Court of Australia in *Smith* was expressly not limited to acts in the commission of the offence which were causally related to the injuries received. It extended to acts done in the commission of the offence, even though the immediate cause of the injuries was not in itself an element of the illegality. So in *Ashton v. Turner* [1981] Q.B. 137, the plaintiff and defendant committed a burglary and in the course of departing from the scene of the crime the car crashed and the plaintiff was injured. Ewbank J., following *Smith*, held that as a matter of public policy the law did not recognise that the defendant owed the plaintiff a duty of care in relation to an act done in connection with the commission of the crime in which they were jointly participating. (See also *Winnik v. Dick* (1984) S.L.T. 185).

Subsequently, a differently constituted High Court of Australia held, by a majority, that it would be wrong to regard *Smith* as authority for the proposition that in all circumstances the participation of plaintiff and defendant in a joint illegal enterprise would negate the existence of a duty of care on the part of the defendant to the plaintiff, even where the alleged breach of arises in the execution of the criminal act.

In *Progress and Properties Ltd v. Craft* (1976) 135 C.L.R. 651 the plaintiff, a workman on a building under construction, was injured when a goods hoist upon which he was being carried fell to the ground. The operator of the hoist was in breach of a regulation in allowing the plaintiff to ride on the hoist and the plaintiff was in breach of the same regulation in riding on the hoist. The plaintiff and the operator were, therefore, jointly engaged in an illegal enterprise. Nevertheless, the plaintiff recovered damages arising from the negligent operation of the hoist. It was held by a majority (Stephen, Mason, Jacobs and Murphy JJ., Barwick C.J. dissenting) that joint illegal activity may extinguish a duty of care which would otherwise be owed by one party to another where the nature of the illegal activity is such that a court cannot or will not establish a standard of care. Here, however, it was held that there was no reason why the Court should not determine a standard of care owed by the operator of the hoist to the plaintiff, because it could be determined without reference to the illegality. Moreover, the regulation which created the illegality was for the benefit of one of the participants in the illegal enterprise.

Likewise, in *Jackson v. Harrison* (1978) 138 C.L.R. 438, recovery was allowed for injuries received by the plaintiff as a result of the defendant's driving even though they were joint participants in an illegal activity. They had been taking it in turns to drive a car, both of their licences being suspended at the time. The majority (Mason, Jacobs, Murphy and Aickin JJ.) took the view that not every case in which the parties had acted together in a manner which was illegal was necessarily subject to the same considerations of public policy. It was necessary to look at the particular offence in question and assess its nature, form and gravity. (See also *Preston v. Dowell* (1987) 45 S.A.S.R. 111 at 122–123 and *George v. Dowling* (1992) 59 S.A.S.R. 291 at 298). In Jacobs J.'s view the facts were such that the joint illegality had no bearing at all on the standard of care reasonably to be expected of the driver. Barwick CJ, however, doubted whether the courts could or should distinguish between criminal offences. He said that it was difficult in logic to place any criminal offence outside the policy which found its expression in *Smith v. Jenkins*.

In *Pitts v. Hunt* [1991] 1 Q.B. 24 (noted by Hopkins (1991) 50 Camb. L.J. 27 and Williams (1991) 54 M.L.R. 745) the English Court of Appeal held that, where the plaintiff was injured as the result of the actions of the defendant while they were engaged in a joint illegal enterprise, the issue whether the plaintiff was entitled to claim against the defendant was to be determined not according to whether there was any moral turpitude involved in the joint illegal enterprise but whether the conduct of the plaintiff seeking to base his claim on the unlawful act and the character of the enterprise and the hazards necessarily inherent in its execution were such that it was impossible to determine the appropriate standard of care because the joint illegal purpose had displaced the ordinary standard of care. See also the discussion in Kidner, "The variable standard of care, contributory negligence and *volenti*" (1991) 11 *Legal Studies* 1 at pp. 18–21.

More recently the *Smith v. Jenkins* principle has once again been re-examined by the High Court of Australia. In *Gala v. Preston* (1991) 172 C.L.R. 243, the Court had to consider whether, where a person was injured because of the negligent driving of an associate while engaged in the joint criminal activity of "joyriding" in a car they had stolen, a duty of care arose. In their joint judgment, Mason C.J., Deane, Gaudron and McHugh JJ. held that, on examination of the relationship between the parties, the joint illegal activity was the only relevant relationship between the parties and that they could have had no reasonable basis for expecting that the car would be driven according to ordinary standards of competence and care. They felt that, in the circumstances of the case before them, it was neither possible nor feasible for a court to determine what was an appropriate standard of care to be expected of the driver. The other judges, however, were more critical of the reasoning in *Jackson v. Harrison*. Brennan J. said that in *Smith v. Jenkins*, the Court had advanced no qualification to the principle that the joint participation in the commission of a criminal offence precluded either of the participants from recovering from the other damages for injuries received in the performance of the offence. Given the unqualified form in which the principle was stated, its application by Barwick C.J. in the two later cases was, to his mind, "logically compelling", although "Draconian in its application". He could not accept, however, the reasoning of Jacobs J. in *Jackson v. Harrison*, that a plaintiff would only fail when the character of the enterprise in which the parties were engaged was such that it was impossible for the court to determine the relevant standard of care. He said at 269:

> Even if one takes the illustration of the safe-blowing burglars, it is not hard to see that, on any standard, it is careless for the burglar with the plunger to detonate the charge while the other is attaching the gelignite to the safe. A standard of care can be determined, albeit the standard is that of the reasonable safe-blower and is attenuated by the exigencies of the crime. . . .

The approach he preferred to adopt was to ask "why should a plaintiff's participation in a defendant's commission of an offence prevent a duty of care to the plaintiff from arising?". In broad terms, he said, it was "because the civil law cannot condone breaches of the criminal law". He continued at 271:

> Where the plaintiff and the defendant respectively engage in conduct in breach of the criminal law and their relationship in engaging in that conduct would, apart from the illegality, give rise to a duty of care owed by the one to the other, the question whether the admitting of that duty of care condones the breach depends, in my view, on the nature of the offence. It is necessary to distinguish between offences which preclude the admission of a duty of care in respect of what is done by the plaintiff and defendant in committing or attempting to commit them and offences which do not preclude the admission of such a duty of care. The distinction is necessary not only to avoid the reproach of a Draconian rule but also to reflect the reality that the admitting of a duty of care in respect of conduct in breach of some laws does not condone their breach. It is only where the admission of a duty of care impairs the normative influence of the law creating an offence that the civil law can be said to condone a breach of that law. In such cases, it would be contrary to public policy to admit a duty of care as between co-offenders in the commission of the offence.

Dawson J. was of a similar view, although he did not wish to confine the policy of refusing to condone the commission of an offence by linking it with the preservation of the normative effect of the criminal law. It was only where (as in *Jackson v. Harrison*) setting the appropriate standard of care did not involve any dependence upon the nature of the criminal activity in which the parties were engaged, that a plaintiff could succeed. Toohey J. was likewise reluctant to lend the law's support to the recovery of damages by "a plaintiff who suffers injury while participating with the defendant in the commission of a serious criminal act, when that act is the act relied upon to found a cause of action" (at 292). A duty of care was held not to exist, not because of any difficulty of defining a standard of care, but "because of the participation by the parties in the criminal activity which resulted in the injury."

Gala v. Preston was applied by the New South Wales Court of Appeal in *Fabre v. Arenales* (1992) 27 N.S.W.L.R. 437, where it was held that, where a driver of a motor vehicle and its passenger were both attempting to escape from the police after both were involved in a criminal offence, the ordinary relationship of proximity, between a driver and a passenger, was transformed into one which lacked the relevant duty to take ordinary care in driving. See also the decision of the Federal Court of Australia in *Italiano v. Barbaro* (1993) 114 A.L.R. 21.

A different approach, however, was taken by the majority of the Supreme Court of Canada when the issue came before it in *Hall v. Herbert* (1993) 101 D.L.R. (4th) 129 (noted

(1994) 110 L.Q.R. 357). McLachlin J., with whom La Forest, L'Heureux-Dube and Iacobucci JJ. concurred, said that the relationship between a plaintiff and a defendant which gave rise to their respective entitlement and liability arose from "a duty predicated on foreseeable consequence of harm". The illegality of the conduct engaged in by both plaintiff and defendant was an extrinsic factor to be considered by way of defence "rather than by distorting the notion of the duty of care owed by the defendant".

Wrongs to unborn child

58.—For the avoidance of doubt it is hereby declared that the law relating to wrongs shall apply to an unborn child for his protection in like manner as if the child were born, provided the child is subsequently born alive.

GENERAL NOTE

This section provides that the law relating to wrongs will apply to an unborn child provided that the child is born alive, thus overruling the decision of the Irish Court of Appeal in *Walker v. Great Northern Railway Company* (1891) 28 L.R. Ir. 69. McMahon and Binchy (*op. cit.* at p.605) are of the view that it is not necessary that the child be viable: "postnatal birth of even momentary duration will suffice". *Quaere*, as do McMahon and Binchy (*ibid.*), whether damages may be recoverable in tort in respect of a wrong committed on an unborn child where the child is not subsequently born alive?

Liability of Minister for Finance for negligent use of mechanically propelled vehicle

59.—(1) Where a wrong is committed by the use of a mechanically propelled vehicle belonging to the State, the Minister for Finance shall be liable to an action for damages in respect of damage resulting from the wrong in like manner as if the Minister for Finance were the owner of the vehicle, and the person using the vehicle shall, for the purposes of such liability, be deemed to be the servant of the Minister for Finance in so far as such person was acting in the course of his duty or employment.

(2) Proceedings may be brought against the Minister for Finance by virtue of this section without obtaining the fiat of the Attorney General.

(3) Nothing in this section shall operate to relieve any person from liability in respect of damage resulting from his own wrong.

(4) For the purposes of this section, a mechanically propelled vehicle not belonging to the State shall—

 (a) while being used when it is under seizure by a person in the service of the State in the course of his duty or employment, or

 (b) while being used by a member of the Garda Siochana or an officer of any Minister for the purpose of a test, removal or disposition of the vehicle pursuant to the Road Traffic Act 1961, or any regulation thereunder

be deemed to belong to the State.

(5) In this section—

"mechanically propelled vehicle" means a vehicle intended or adapted for propulsion by mechanical means, including—

 (a) a bicycle or tricycle, with an attachment for propelling it by mechanical power, whether or not the attachment is being used,

(b) a vehicle the means of propulsion of which is electrical or partly electrical and partly mechanical;

"use" includes keeping or leaving stationary.

GENERAL NOTE

This section was one of a number of legislative inroads into the doctrine of sovereign immunity, which doctrine was itself subsequently swept away by the Supreme Court in *Byrne v. Ireland* [1972] I.R. 241. Consequently, in the case of a person injured by the negligent use of a mechanically propelled vehicle belonging to the State, where that vehicle was used in the course of employment of a State employee, the aggrieved party may either sue the Minister for Finance by virtue of this section or the State itself under the principle enunciated in *Byrne*: see further Hogan and Kerr, "The Law of Ireland" in Bradley and Bell (eds.), *Governmental Liability: A Comparative Study* (UKNCCL, 1991), pp. 155–156. It would also seem to be permissible to sue both the Minister for Finance and Ireland; see, *e.g. Murray v. Minister for Finance, Ireland and the Attorney General*, Supreme Court, April 21, 1982 (reproduced in McMahon and Binchy, *A Casebook on the Irish Law of Torts* (1983), p. 80).

Subsection (2) is now unnecessary since the general requirement in section 2(1) of the Ministers and Secretaries Act 1924 that one had to obtain the fiat of the Attorney General before one could sue a Minister was condemned on constitutional grounds by Kenny J. in *Macauley v. Minister for Posts and Telegraphs* [1966] I.R. 345.

Liability of road authority for failure to maintain public road

60.—(1) A road authority shall be liable for damage caused as a result of their failure to maintain adequately a public road.

(2) In proceedings under this section, it shall be a defence for the road authority to prove that—

(a) they had given sufficient warning that the road was a danger to traffic, or

(b) they had taken reasonable precautions to secure that the road was not a danger to traffic, or

(c) they had not a reasonable opportunity to give such warning or take such precautions, or

(d) the damage resulted from a wrong committed by any person other than the road authority.

(3) In determining whether a road was adequately maintained, regard shall be had in particular to—

(a) the construction of the road and the standard of maintenance appropriate to a road of such construction,

(b) the traffic using the road,

(c) the condition in which a reasonable person would have expected to find the road.

(4) In determining whether a road authority had a reasonable opportunity to give warning that a road was a danger to traffic or had taken reasonable precautions to secure that a road was not such a danger, regard shall be had to the standard of supervision reasonable for a road of such character.

(5) In this section—

"road authority" means the council of a county, the corporation of a county or other borough and the council of an urban district, "public road" means a road the responsibility for the maintenance of which lies on a road authority and includes any bridge, pipe, arch, gulley, footway, pavement, fence, railing or wall which forms part of such road and which it is the responsibility of the road authority to maintain.

(6) This section shall not apply to damage arising from an event which occurred before the coming into operation of this section.

(7) This section shall come into operation on such day, not earlier than the 1st day of April, 1967, as may be fixed therefor by order made by the Government.

GENERAL NOTE

Subsection (1) provides that a local authority shall be liable for damage caused as a result of its failure to adequately maintain public roads. At common law, a highway authority was not liable for injury or loss caused by its failure to maintain a public road in proper repair. Nor is it under a duty to exercise reasonable care in the control and management of such a road even with respect to known dangers: see *Cowley v. Newmarket Local Board* [1892] A.C. 345. The principle that a local authority is not liable for an injury to a user of the highway resulting from its failure to repair an be traced back to *Russell v. The Men Dwelling in the County of Devon* (1788) 2 T.R. 667. The basis of the immunity is that at common law the duty of repairing highways fell on the community. By virtue of a statute of 1612 (11, 12 and 13 Jac. 1, c. 7 (Ir)), this duty was imposed on the parish. Because the inhabitants were not a corporation they could not be sued collectively and therefore no action lay against them in respect of their failure to carry out their duty. Despite the changes wrought by the Local Government (Ireland) Act 1898 — most notably the imposition by section 2, on every county and district council, of the duty of keeping the roads in good repair — the position remained the same: see *Harbinson v. Armagh County Council* [1902] 2 I.R. 538.

The position is otherwise where the authority repairs the highway in a negligent manner: see *Clements v. Tyrone County Council* [1905] 2 I.R. 415. Highway authorities "are liable in damages for injuries suffered by a road user if they have been negligent in doing repairs or in interfering with the road. They are not liable for injuries suffered or caused by want of repair of a road. This is the familiar distinction, they are liable for misfeasance but not for non-feasance. The distinction between non-feasance and misfeasance has been judicially described as "unsatisfactory" (*per* Kingsmill Moore J. in *Kelly v. Mayo County Council* [1964] I.R. 315 at 324) and "anomalous" (*per* Murnaghan J. in *O'Brien v. Waterford County Council* [1926] I.R. 1 at 8) but was regarded by the legislature as being sufficiently well established to warrant its abrogation by statute. See, however, Bland's interesting thesis that the non-feasance defence was abolished by the Occupiers' Liability Act 1995: "The Strange Death of the Nonfeasance Defence" (1998) 16 I.L.T. (N.S.) 172.

Subsection (7) however, provides that the section is to come into operation on such day, not earlier than 1 April 1967, as might be fixed by order of the Government. No such order has yet been made. In *State (Sheehan) v. Government of Ireland* [1987] I.R. 550, Costello J. held that the government had failed in its statutory duty and made an order of mandamus directed against the government compelling them to bring section 60 into effect saying (at 556):

> If Parliament intended (as I think clearly it did) that the law should be reformed, it did not intend to confer a discretion which would permit that intention to be frustrated. This means that the discretion given by subs. (7) is a limited one and that it should be construed as requiring the government to make an order with reasonable time after the 1st April, 1967. Obviously a reasonable time has long since passed and in my opinion the Government is shown to have failed to carry out the duty imposed upon it by the section.

A majority of the Supreme Court, however, took a different view, with Henchy J. (Finlay C.J., Griffin and Hederman JJ. concurring, McCarthy J. dissenting) holding in effect that the discretion vested in the Government was unreviewable. He observed that subsection (7) provided that the section was to come into force on such day as may (and not shall) be fixed by the Government and concluded at 561:

> the important law reform to be effected by the section was not to take effect unless and until the government became satisfied that, in the light of factors such as the necessary deployment of financial and other resources, the postulated reform could be carried into effect. The discretion vested in the Government to bring the section into operation on a date after April 1, 1967, was not limited in any way, as to time or otherwise.

On *Sheehan*, see generally Hogan (1987) 9 D.U.L.J. (N.S.) 91.

Given recent developments in the law on civil liability, it is possible that the Irish courts would react favourably to arguments that local authorities were not immune from liability in respect of non-feasance: see *Forsyth v. Evans* [1980] N.I. 230. In any event, as noted above, the immunity can only be claimed for non-feasance, not for loss or injury caused by misfeasance. To be liable for misfeasance the highway authority must not only have done something to the road, but in so doing must have created or added to a danger in the road. So, where a highway authority does work by way of repair on a road and the work is properly done but not sufficient to remove the danger, the authority will not be liable for injury resulting from the danger: see *Burton v. West Suffolk County Council* [1960] 1 Q.B. 72. If, however, the authority carries out repairs negligently in such a way as to create, or add to, a danger it will be liable for any loss or injury suffered as a consequence.

There would also appear to be a number of other exceptions to the rule. Under the device of the "source of authority" test the plaintiff may be able to establish liability if it can be shown that the authority was acting in a capacity other than as a highway authority: see *Buckle v. Bayswater Road Board* (1936) 57 C.L.R. 259, where the defendant was held to be acting as a drainage authority, and *Hayes v. Brisbane City Council* (1980) 5 Q.L. 269. In this latter case, the plaintiff sustained injuries alighting from a bus at a bus stop because the surrounds had not been properly maintained. Judge McGuire held that the Council, through its transportation department, had failed in their duty of care owed to bus passengers. Furthermore he found that the Council was acting in a dual capacity and could be held liable when acting in its capacity of a transport authority. Likewise the "artificial structure" test is another means of avoiding the rule. The origin of this device is regarded as being the Privy Council's decision in *Borough of Bathurst v. Macpherson* (1879) 4 App. Cas. 256. In that case, in issue was the liability for a defective drain which the borough had constructed in the road. Sir Barnes Peacock, delivering the judgment of their Lordships, said at 265:

> the duty was cast upon them of keeping the artificial work which they had created in such a state as to prevent it causing a danger to passengers on the highway which, but for such artificial construction, would not have existed.

See also *Webb v. The State of South Australia* (1982) 56 A.L.J.R. 912.

If and when the section is implemented, the plaintiff will have to prove that the damage of which he or she complains was caused as a result of the authority's failure to maintain adequately a public road. In determining whether the road was adequately maintained particular regard is to be had to the matters set out in subsection (3). The term "public road" is widely defined in subsection (5). It would seem that the plaintiff need not prove that the authority had been guilty of lack of reasonable care. Subsection (2), however, provides that it will be a defence for the authority to show, *inter alia*, that it had taken reasonable precautions to secure that the road was not a danger to traffic.

By shifting what Fleming has described as the "burden of excuse" on the authority, the section actually imposes a liability stricter than negligence. It can be argued that the shift is justifiable on the ground that the authority will have better access to the kind of information that would enable a court to determine whether reasonable care had been taken.

Proof of claims for damages or contribution in bankruptcy

61.—(1) Notwithstanding any other enactment or any rule of law, a claim for damages or contribution in respect of a wrong shall be provable in bank-ruptcy where the wrong out of which the liability to damages or the right to contribution arose was committed before the time of the bankruptcy.

(2) Where the damages or contribution have not been and cannot be other-wise liquidated or ascertained, the court may make such order as to it seems fit for the assessment of the damages or contribution, and the amount when so assessed shall be provable as if it were a debt due at the time of the bankruptcy.

(3) Where a claim for contribution or in respect of a judgment debt for contribution is provable in bankruptcy, no such proof shall be admitted except to the extent that the claimant has satisfied the debt or damages of the injured person, unless the injured person does not prove in respect of the wrong or debt.

GENERAL NOTE

This section provides, in subsection (1), that all claims for damages or contribution will be provable in bankruptcy where the wrong out of which the liability to damages or the right to contribution arose was committed before the time of the bankruptcy. The section is not affected by the Bankruptcy Act 1988 and the court before which the claim for damages is being made may, by virtue of subsection (2), make an order "for the assessment of the damages or contribution and the amount so assessed shall be provable as if it were a debt due at the time of the bankruptcy", notwithstanding that the assessment takes place after adjudication.

Subsection (3) provides that, where a claim for contribution or in respect of a judgment debt for contribution is provable in bankruptcy, no such proof shall be admitted except to the extent that the claimant has satisfied the debt or damages of the injured person, unless the injured person does not prove in respect of the wrong or debt.

Section 75(3) of the Bankruptcy Act 1988 provides that where "all necessary parties agree, an order for assessment of damages or contribution under section 61(2) of the Civil Liability Act 1961 may be made by the Court, notwithstanding that it may not be the court by or before which the claim for damages or contribution falls to be determined."

Application of moneys payable under certain policies of insurance

62.—Where a person (hereinafter referred to as the insured) who has ef-fected a policy of insurance in respect of liability for a wrong, if an individual, becomes a bankrupt or dies or, if a corporate body, is wound up or, if a partner-ship or other unincorporated association, is dissolved, moneys payable to the insured under the policy shall be applicable only to discharging in full all valid claims against the insured in respect of which those moneys are payable, and no part of those moneys shall be assets of the insured or applicable to the payment of the debts (other than those claims) of the insured in the bankruptcy or in the administration of the estate of the insured or in the winding-up or dissolution, and no such claim shall be provable in the bankruptcy, administra-tion, winding-up or dissolution.

GENERAL NOTE

In *Dunne v. P.J. White Construction Co. Ltd* [1989] I.L.R.M. 803, Finlay C.J., with whom Henchy, Griffin, Hederman and McCarthy JJ. agreed, said that this section was spe-cifically designed to protect an injured plaintiff whose defendant had died, gone bankrupt or gone into liquidation so as to ensure that monies payable on a policy of insurance to the defendant "will not be eaten up by other creditors, but will go to satisfy his compensation". Although a full debate on the point had not taken place it seemed that an inevitable consequence of the terms of the section was that the injured person had the right to bring an action against the defendant's insurers. The Supreme Court also ruled that the injured person had the benefit of the presumption that the defendant's insurance policy was good. To properly implement the protection given by the section it was necessary that the onus of proving the existence of a right to rescind or repudiate the policy lay on the insurers.

The section is not affected by the provisions of the Bankruptcy Act 1988: see Sanfey and Holohan, *Bankruptcy Law and Practice in Ireland* (1991, The Round Hall Press), p.166.

Costs in certain actions in which the plaintiff is an infant

63.—(1) Where a sum of money has been lodged in court by the defendant in an action for a wrong in which the plaintiff is an infant, an application may be made to the judge by the plaintiff to decide whether that sum of money should be accepted or the action should go to trial and–

(a) if, on any such application, the judge decides that the action should go to trial, and

(b) an amount by way of damages is awarded to the plaintiff which does not exceed the sum so lodged,

then, notwithstanding any rule of court or practice to the contrary, the costs in the action shall be at the discretion of the judge.

(2) An appeal shall lie from the order of the judge in relation to the costs in such action.

GENERAL NOTE

Under the Rules of the Superior Courts 1986, Ord. 22, r. 10 an infant plaintiff cannot accept money lodged in court by the defendant with his defence without the approval of the court. Before the Act came into operation and an infant plaintiff applied to the court for such approval the court, in approving of acceptance, relied almost entirely on the recommendations of counsel for the infant plaintiff that in counsel's considered opinion the sum lodged should be withdrawn on behalf of the plaintiff. If the court approved acceptance it would award costs against the defendant to the date of lodgment together with the costs of the application to approve. Where the court, notwithstanding counsel's opinion, declined to approve, the action would go to trial and, if the amount did not exceed the lodgment, the infant plaintiff suffered the consequences of having not only to pay the defendant's costs of the action incurred subsequent to the date of lodgment but also the plaintiff's own costs: the Rules of the Superior Courts 1986, Ord. 22, r. 6. Now the judge, notwithstanding that the amount recovered does not exceed the amount of the lodgment may, in his or her discretion, allow the infant plaintiff the costs of the action: see *Shanley v. Casey* [1967] I.R. 338, 345–346 *per* Budd J. Speaking extra-judicially, Murnaghan J. (SYS Lecture No. 36, November 3, 1968) has pointed out that in those cases which went to trial under section 63, it was the trial judge who exercised the discretion. However, on a strict interpretation of the section, he thought the discretion was given to the judge who decided that the action should go to trial.

Murnaghan J. went on to say that there was good reason for providing that an infant who must apply to the court for approval should not suffer in costs if it subsequently turned out that the judge to whom such application was made mistakenly withheld approval. He found it difficult to accept however, that, where a judge turns out to have been mistaken, it would be just to deprive a defendant, who had lodged more than sufficient to satisfy the plaintiff's claim, of his costs or to order him to pay the plaintiff's costs:

> If the infant is, in the discretion of the judge, to be exempted from the ordinary rule then . . . provision should have been for the payment of any costs involved in the exercise of that discretion out of state funds. I cannot see why a defendant who has

done everything he can do, namely lodged a sum in court which is more than sufficient to compensate the plaintiff, should be made to pay for a mistake made by a
judge on an application to which such defendant was not even a party.

In *Bourke v. Corás Iompair Éireann* [1967] I.R. 319, Ó Dálaigh C.J., with whom Haugh
and Walsh JJ. agreed, described section 63 as "a kind of pre-trial provision for the assistance
of infant plaintiffs". It provides a means whereby an infant plaintiff is enabled to obtain from
a judge a decision as to whether a lodgment made in an action should be accepted or whether
the action should go to trial. The object is to safeguard the infant plaintiff.

In this case the defendants had lodged £1,380 in court. The plaintiff and his father were
content to accept this but counsel advised against. The plaintiff issued a notice of motion for
an order in the terms of section 63 deciding whether the sum lodged should be accepted or
whether the action should go for trial. Murnaghan J. refused. He said he would not consider
any application unless counsel for the applicant stated that he recommended the acceptance
of the sum lodged. To do otherwise would lead, he thought, to very great abuse. In his
opinion the situation contemplated by the section was where counsel urged the court to give
its approval and the court refused but, as subsequently, transpired, erroneously refused. It
did not envisage that counsel could move an application hoping it would be refused. The
Supreme Court disagreed and said that this was too narrow a view of the purpose and ambit
of section 63:

> It has to be borne in mind that the section is enacted for the protection of the inter-
> ests of an infant plaintiff. Applications under the section are not limited in any way.
> There is no requirement that the plaintiff's counsel shall approve acceptance of the
> lodgment or that the infant plaintiff or next friend shall approve. . . . Now the infant
> plaintiff can have an objective consideration of the position before trial and a deci-
> sion whether he should accept or go to trial. The section clearly contemplates that
> the judge's ruling will be binding – requiring acceptance or to got to trial as the case
> may be. It is therefore the applicant's duty to furnish the judge with as much assist-
> ance as he may require for his decision. The judge may properly take into account
> counsel's opinion and the reasons he gives for it. That counsel is of the opinion that
> the lodgment is inadequate is no more than a factor to be taken into account by the
> judge.

In other words the judge to whom a section 63 application is made has a much more
positive role to play than before. The judge is now required to make an objective decision.

In *Ennis v. McKenna Distributors Ltd*, unreported, High Court, November 19, 1965, an
application under section 63 was made to Murnaghan J. The infant plaintiff had suffered
severe personal injuries as a result of which it was necessary to be able to say what was the
prognosis for the infant's future. The sum lodged in court was approximately £5,000.
Murnaghan J. felt unable to come to a conclusion on the application without seeing and
hearing the infant and his doctors. Having heard oral evidence he decided that the action
should go to trial. In the event there was no trial because the defendant subsequently made
an increased offer. On a fresh application for the court's approval, Murnaghan J. was of the
opinion that the new offer should be accepted. Difficulties arose however in relation to the
costs of the oral hearing, including the witness expenses of the doctors.

Murnaghan J. was not persuaded that it was proper to order the defendant to pay these
costs and therefore he made no order. Subsequently a similar issue came before the Supreme
Court in *Shanley v. Casey* [1967] I.R. 338. Murnaghan J. had decided that a section 63
application in which the judge decided that the action should go to trial was an unsuccessful
application and that therefore the applicant was not entitled to costs. The Supreme Court,
however, held that the costs and expenses of a section 63 application were costs and expenses reasonably incurred for the purpose of the proceedings within the contemplation of
what is now the Rules of the Superior Courts 1986, Ord. 99, r. 1.

It should be noted that the Rules of the Superior Courts 1986, Ord. 22, r. 10 go further
than section 63 in that the Rule applies equally to persons of unsound mind and covers not
just the acceptance of money lodged in court, but also settlements and compromises.

SCHEDULE

ENACTMENTS REPEALED

PART I

Acts of the Parliament of England applied to Ireland by the Act of the Parliament of Ireland (10 Henry 7. c. 22 (Ir.)) passed in the year 1495 and entitled "An Act confirming all Statutes made in England"

Session and Chapter (1)	Title (2)	Extent of Repeal (3)
13 Edw. 1 (Stat. Westm. sec.), c. 23	Writ of accompt for executors (1285)	The whole chapter
4. Edw. 3. c. 7.	Executors shall have an action of trespass for a wrong done to their testator (1330)	The whole chapter

PART II

ACT OF THE PARLIAMENT OF IRELAND

Session and Chapter (1)	Title (2)	Extent of Repeal (3)
10 Chas. 1. sess. 2. c.5 (Ir.).	An Act for the recovery of arrearages of rents by executors of tenant in fee simple (1634)	The whole Act so far as unrepealed

PART III

ACTS OF THE PARLIAMENT OF THE LATE UNITED KINGDOM OF GREAT BRITAIN AND IRELAND

Session and Chapter (1)	Short Title (2)	Extent of Repeal (3)
3 & 4 Vict. c.105	Debtors (Ireland) Act 1840	Section 31
51 & 52 Vic. c.64	Law of Libel Amendment Act 1888	Section 5
1 & 2 Geo. 5. c.57	Maritime Conventions Act 1911	Sections 1, 2, 8, 3, 8 and 9

PART IV

ACT OF THE OIREACHTAS OF SAORSTÁT ÉIREANN

Number and Year (1)	Short Title (2)	Extent of Repeal (3)
No. 40 of 1936	Air Navigation and Transport Act 1936	Section 23

PART V

ACTS OF THE OIREACHTAS

Number and Year (1)	Short Title (2)	Extent of Repeal (3)
No. 1 of 1951	Tortfeasors Act 1951	The whole Act
No. 3 of 1956	Fatal Injuries Act 1956	The whole Act
No. 6 of 1957	Statute of Limitations 1957	Subsection (3) of section 2, and subparagraph (iii) of paragraph (e) of subsection (1) and subsection (3) of section 11.
No. 1 of 1959	Air Navigation and Transport Act 1959	Section 4
No. 24 of 1961	Road Traffic Act 1961	Subsection (4) of section 76 and section 116 and 117

CIVIL LIABILITY (AMENDMENT) ACT 1964

(1964 No. 17)

ARRANGEMENT OF SECTIONS

1. Principal Act.
2. Sums not to be taken into account in assessing damages (personal injury not causing death).
3. Amendment of section 27 of Principal Act.
4. Amendment of section 35(2) of Principal Act.
5. Amendment of section 36 of Principal Act.
6. Repeals.
7. Short title, construction and collective citation.
    Schedule.

An Act to amend and extend the Civil Liability Act 1961. [*7th July* 1964]

INTRODUCTION

This Act amends and extends the 1961 Act. According to the Minister for Justice (Vol. 211 *Dáil Debates* col. 581) it had three main objects. First, it abolished the need for certain special findings by the judge or jury in a contributory negligence case; secondly, it continued as a permanent part of the law the temporary provision in the 1961 Act enabling compensation for mental distress to be awarded in fatal injuries cases; thirdly, it provides that, in assessing damages in a non fatal case, account is not to be taken of any sum payable under a contract of insurance of any pension gratuity or other like benefit payable in consequence of the injury.

Principal Act

1.—In this Act "the Principal Act" means the Civil Liability Act 1961.

Sums not to be taken into account in assessing damages (personal injury not causing death)

2.—In assessing damages in an action to recover damages in respect of a wrongful act (including a crime) resulting in personal injury not causing death, account shall not be taken of-
  (a) any sum payable in respect of the injury under any contract of insurance,
  (b) any pension, gratuity or other like benefit payable under statute or otherwise in consequence of the injury.

GENERAL NOTE

This provision is similar to that applicable to wrongful death actions in section 50 of the 1961 Act. White, *op. cit.*, p. 208, submits that the rule of non-deduction prescribed by the section is "probably only applicable to money payments", but see *Liffen v. Watson* [1940] K.B. 556, in which the English Court of Appeal held that provision by the plaintiff's father of board and lodging should be ignored in the assessment of damages, which included damages for having lost employment which provided board and lodging. Geoghegan J., in *Greene v. Hughes Haulage Ltd* [1997] 3 I.R. 109 at 117, was of the opinion that the "whole purpose" of section 2 "was to provide a corresponding statutory provision for personal injury actions to section 50 [of the 1961 Act] which provided for equivalent non-deductions in fatal injury claims". Consequently it seemed to the learned judge to be reasonable to assume that section 2 "was intended by the Oireachtas to be interpreted similarly to section 50 of the 1961 Act". As Geoghegan J. pointed out "the question of non deductibility of insurance monies in a personal injury claim as distinct from a fatal injury claim was until 1964 in Ireland and still is in England governed solely by the common law and not by statute". Note that in Scotland the position is regulated by statute: Administration of Justice Act 1992, section 10 on which see *Lewicki v. Brown & Root Wimpey Highland Fabricators Ltd* [1996] I.R.L.R. 565.

The original leading case was *Bradburn v. Great Western Railway Co* (1874) L.R. 10 Ex. 1, in which it was held that payments received for loss of wages pursuant to a private policy of insurance should not be deducted from the lost wages claim of a plaintiff. The explanation of the *Bradburn* principle was put thus by Lord Reid in *Parry v. Cleaver* [1970] A.C. 1 at 14:

> As regards monies coming to the plaintiff under a contract of insurance, I think that the real and substantial reason for disregarding them is that the plaintiff has bought them and that it would be unjust and unreasonable to hold that the money which he prudently spent on premiums and the benefit from it should inure to the benefit of the tort-feasor. Here again I think that the explanation that this is too remote is artificial and unreal. Why should the plaintiff be left worse off than if he had never insured? In that case he would have got the benefit of the premium money : if he had not spent it, he would have had it in his possession at the time of the accident grossed up at compound interest.

The principle first set out in *Bradburn* and adopted in *Parry v. Cleaver*, was affirmed by the High Court of Australia in *Graham v. Baker* (1961) 106 C.L.R. 340 and by the Supreme Court of Canada in *Guy v. Trizec Equities Ltd* (1979) 99 D.L.R. (3d) 243 at 247–248. See also Lord Templeman in *Smoker v. London Fire and Civil Defence Authority* [1991] 2 A.C. 502 at 544. Geoghegan J. noted in *Greene* that, "despite this clear exposition", the authorities were confused as to when collateral benefits were to be deducted (citing *Payne v. Railway Executive* [1952] 1 K.B. 26; *Browning v. War Office* [1963] 1 Q.B. 750 and *Parsons v. BNM Laboratories Ltd* [1964] 1 Q.B. 95) and speculated that it "may well have been because of the uncertainty of the common law at that time that the Oireachtas decided to enact section 2 [of the 1964 Act] simplifying the position and in effect applying to personal injury actions the same rules as to non deductibility as already applied to fatal injury actions under section 50 [of the 1961 Act]." For an example of the continuing uncertainty in England, see the contrasting views of the Court of Appeal and the House of Lords in *Longden v. British Coal Corporation* [1995] I.C.R. 957 and [1998] I.C.R. 26.

Greene raised the question of whether monies of which the plaintiff was, and would continue to be, in receipt pursuant to a policy of insurance taken out by her former employers should be deducted from her loss of earnings. The company had an employee benefit plan designed to provide not just a retirement pension, but also an income in the event of long-term injury or illness. Under the plan, when the employee was totally disabled for a continuous period of six months, an income was paid by the insurance company equal to 75 per cent of the salary at the date of disablement, inclusive of the basic social welfare disability benefit. The income was to be paid until recovery, death, or reaching normal pension date and would increase during payment at the rate of 5 per cent *per annum* compound. The defendant submitted that the insurance policy made with the employer was not a contract of insurance of the kind contemplated by section 2 of the 1964 Act because of the fact that the premiums were paid by the employer. Geoghegan J. held, however, that the payments made by the insurance company to the plaintiff were payments made in respect of the injury under a contract of insurance and, even though the plaintiff was not a party to the contract of insurance, the contract of insurance was made for her benefit. Consequently, the disability payments already paid or to be paid were not deducted.

Geoghegan J. went on to express the opinion that, even if the common law position pertained, a strong argument could have been made in favour of non-deductibility, a view supported by the majority decision of the Supreme Court of Canada in *Cooper v. Miller* (1994) 113 D.L.R. (4th) 1. See also the unreported decision of McDermott L.J. in *Guy v. Police Authority for Northern Ireland*, April 14, 1989.

In *McKenna v. Best Travel Ltd*, unreported, High Court, December 17, 1996, Lavan J. was dealing with a case where the plaintiff suffered personal injury while on holiday in Israel. One of the issues with which the learned judge had to deal was whether money received by the plaintiff from the Israeli government as victim impact compensation should be deducted from the sum claimed by the plaintiff. Having considered the position both under statute and at common law, he determined that it should not.

Paragraph (a) confirms the common law rule that payments made in pursuance of an insurance policy are to be ignored in assessing the plaintiff's damages: see *Woodman Matheson & Co. Ltd v. Brennan* (1941) 75 I.L.T.R. 34.

In *Dennehy v. Nordic Cold Storage Ltd*, unreported, High Court, May 8, 1991 (see Appendix One, page 85) an employee, absent from work due to an injury, received a regular payment of monies from his employer pursuant to a non-contributory income protection plan and subsequently sued his employer for loss of earnings. The employer was indemnified, pursuant to a contract of insurance, for the income-continuance payments and the plaintiff argued that section 2 applied and that the monies so paid should not be taken into account. Hamilton P. held that such a contract of insurance did not fall within the section's ambit and that, consequently, the monies received by the employee ought to be deducted from the assessment of damages. In effect, Hamilton P. was prepared to imply the words "to the plaintiff" after the words "any sum payable" in paragraph (a).

Likewise paragraph (b) confirms the common law rule that charitable payments are ignored in the assessment of damages: see Andrews L.C.J. in *Redpath v. Belfast and County Down Railway* [1947] N.I. 167 at 175, who said that "common sense and natural justice" rose in revolt against the proposition that charitable payments should be taken into account. Why, he asked, should a defendant's burden be lightened by the generosity of the public? The rationale for this rule was put thus by McLachlin J. of the Supreme Court of Canada in *Cunningham v. Wheeler* (1994) 113 D.L.R. (4th) 1 at 25:

> If a plaintiff is injured and his neighbour brings him a basket of groceries or donates to him a sum of money, the law will not deduct the value of the basket from the damages which the negligent defendant must pay nor require that the monetary gift be called into account. This exception [to the rule against double recovery] reflects the concern of the courts who initiated it that people should not be discouraged from aiding those in misfortune. Arguably, it also reflects the reality that in most cases it would be more trouble that it is worth to require the court hear evidence and rule on the value of charitable assistance.

Consequently, the position as regards the proceeds of a subscription taken up by neighbours or colleagues to assist an injured plaintiff is quite clear; they would not be taken into account in assessing the damages to be paid by the person who caused the injury. What, however, of the costs of services gratuitously provided by a friend or relative to an injured plaintiff? Can a plaintiff, disabled as a result of another's negligence, recover a sum representing the value of necessary services provided gratuitously by a relative or friend? Both the English Court of Appeal, in *Donnelly v. Joyce* [1974] Q.B. 457, and the High Court of Australia, in *Griffiths v. Kerkemeyer* (1977) 139 C.L.R. 161, answered this last question in the affirmative. In the Australian case the plaintiff, who was rendered a quadriplegic as the result of the negligence of the defendant, recovered damages which included a sum representing the value of nursing and other services gratuitously provided for him in the past and to be provided in the future by his fiancée and members of his family.

In this jurisdiction the matter was touched on by Walsh J. in *Doherty v. Bowaters Irish Wallboard Mills Ltd* [1968] I.R. 277, where the plaintiff, a 30-year-old unmarried man, suffered devastating injuries and the damages awarded included a sum for future attention of an unskilled type, *i.e.* not the attention of a qualified nurse. The plaintiff had been living with his parents at the time of the accident and it had been suggested to the jury that consideration should be given to the prospect that his parents, at least for some considerable portion of their remaining lifetime, would perform tasks of personal attention for the plaintiff. Walsh J. observed at 286 that in his view this was not a factor which should affect the award of damages:

> It is certain that the plaintiff will require attention. If he continues to live with his parents, the fact that his parents, even if able to provide the attention by their own efforts, might be willing to do so is entirely a chance, though it may well be a happy chance for the plaintiff; but, even if such a contingency is in the realms of probability for the limited period of the lifetime of the parents, it does not follow that the plaintiff ought not to or might not, reimburse them or remunerate them to the same extent as he would in the case of other attendants.

See also *Cooke v. Walsh* [1984] I.L.R.M. 208, in which the plaintiff's mother was awarded a sum to provide services for her severely injured child.

Should it make any difference if the services are provided by the defendant tortfeasor? Having provided the services, should the defendant be required to pay, in addition, the cost of providing them? In *Kars v. Kars* (1996) 71 A.L.J.R. 107 (noted by Luntz (1997) 113 L.Q.R. 201), the High Court of Australia held that it did not matter that the carer was the actual tortfeasor. The fact that a defendant fulfilled the function of providing services did not, as such, decrease in the slightest the plaintiff's need. In the view of Toohey, McHugh, Gummow and Kirby JJ., in their joint judgment at 120–121, to deny the plaintiff recovery of the cost of the services gratuitously provided "would not only be unjust to the plaintiff, it would provide the very windfall to the defendant (or, more realistically, his or her insurer) which sustained the original provision of damages for gratuitous service in favour of the plaintiffs". Dawson J., in his separate concurring judgment, expressly focused his conclusion on the fact that the provision of voluntary services was "a benevolence which is prompted by the ties of friendship, or familial concern or duty" and cited Windeyer J. in *National Insurance Co. of New Zealand Ltd v. Espagne* (1961) 105 C.L.R. 569 at 598, that the "most satisfying of the reasons that have been given for refusing to diminish damages because of voluntary gifts is that they are given for the benefit of the sufferer and not for the benefit of the wrongdoer". Dawson J. could see no "relevant distinction" between a financial benefit and a benefit in the form of services.

The issue of whether the voluntary provision of assistance by a defendant tortfeasor precludes a plaintiff from securing sums representing the value of such services came before the English Court of Appeal in *Hunt v. Severs* [1993] Q.B. 815. Sir Thomas Bingham M.R., with whom Staughton and Waite LJJ. concurred, said at 831 that the trial judge had been correct in holding that the plaintiff was not so precluded:

> Where services are voluntarily rendered by a tortfeasor in caring for the plaintiff from motives of affection or duty they should in our opinion be regarded as in the same category as services rendered voluntarily by a third-party, or charitable gifts, or insurance payments. They are adventitious benefits, which for policy reasons are not to be regarded as diminishing the plaintiff's loss.

The House of Lords reversed this decision, holding that the damages awarded to a plaintiff under this heading were held in trust for the voluntary carer and could not be recovered by the tortfeasor: see [1994] 2 A.C. 350 (noted by Kemp (1994) 110 L.Q.R. 524; Mathews and Lunny (1995) 58 M.L.R. 395 and Rees (1995) 15 O.J.L.S. 133). Lord Bridge at 363 said that the underlying rationale was to enable the voluntary carer to receive proper recompense for his or her services. The High Court of Australia, however, in *Kars*, expressly disagreed with this approach and said that the damages were recoverable to compensate the plaintiff for the loss which was evidenced by the need for the services and that it was a matter for the plaintiff as to whether they are used to recompense the person providing the services: see Dawson J. (1996) 71 A.L.J.R. 107 at 109. See also Stephen and Mason JJ. in *Griffiths v. Kerkemeyer* (1977) 139 C.L.R. 101 at 176–177 and 193–194 respectively. For a penetrating analysis of *Kars* see Degeling, "Balancing the Interests of Carers and Victims" (1997) 71 A.L.J. 882. On this issue generally see the English Law Commission's Consultation Paper No. 144, *Damages for Personal Injury: Medical, Nursing and Other Expenses* (1996).

The meaning of the paragraph was considered by Lynch J. in *Honan v. Syntex (Ireland)*

Ltd, unreported, High Court, October 22, 1990, who said that the words "or otherwise" in the phrase "payable under statute or otherwise" had the same general sense as the preceding words and they meant "an obligation imposed upon an employer, whether he likes it or not, that is to say, compulsory obligation, as distinct from an obligation undertaken freely and voluntarily by an employer."

This section would also render all social welfare payments non-deductible, but section 75(1) of the Social Welfare (Consolidation) Act 1993 provides that, notwithstanding section 2, in an action for damages for personal injuries:

> . . . there shall in assessing those damages be taken into account, against any loss of earnings or profits which has accrued or probably will accrue to the injured person from the injuries, the value of any rights which have accrued or will probably accrue to him therefrom in respect of injury benefit (disregarding any right in respect of injury benefit payable by virtue of section 210, after the death of the injured person) or disablement benefit (disregarding any increase thereof under section 57 in respect of constant attendance) for the five years beginning with the time when the cause of action accrued.

In addition, section 237(1) of the 1993 Act provides that, notwithstanding section 2, in assessing damages in any action in respect of liability for personal injuries not causing death relating to the use of a "mechanically propelled vehicle", there shall be taken into account "the value of any rights arising from such injuries which have accrued, or are likely to accrue, to the injured person in respect of disabilities benefit... or invalidity pension... for the period of five years beginning with the time when the cause of action accrued". The predecessor of these provisions, section 12 of the Social Welfare Act 1984, was trenchantly criticised by MacKenzie J. in *O'Loughlin v. Teeling* [1988] I.L.R.M. 617, as being "such a dramatic and unfair piece of legislation as to be contrary to natural justice". It appeared to him "basically unfair that a man getting damages for pain and suffering he underwent should have those damages reduced substantially if not entirely eliminated by reason of benefits paid to him". He concluded by asking as to why the insurance company should take advantage of these payments: "A man who gets disability or disablement benefit is in fact getting his own money back; it strikes me as grossly unfair and to a degree contrary to natural justice to attach the money he is getting for suffering in that manner." The reason is that the Prices Advisory Committee (Motor Insurance) in its *Report of Enquiry into the Cost and Methods of Providing Motor Insurance* (1982) recommended that one of the ways in which motor insurance premiums might be reduced would be to allow a defendant to offset the damages payable by reference to social welfare payments received by the injured plaintiff.

On the relationship between section 2 and Article 93 of Council Regulation 1408/71/ EEC on the application of social security schemes to employed persons and their families moving within the Community, see *Van Keep v. Surface Dressing Contractors Ltd*, unreported, High Court, June 11, 1993 (Budd J.). The treatment of collateral benefits, the policy arguments for and against non-deduction, and the options for reform are extensively considered in the English Law Commission's Consultation Paper No. 147, *Damages for Personal Injury: Collateral Benefits* (1997).

3.—*[Amending section 27 of the Principal Act]*
4.—*[Amending section 35(2) of the Principal Act]*
5.—*[Amending section 36 of the Principal Act]*

Repeals

6.—The enactments mentioned in the Schedule to this Act are hereby repealed to the extent specified in the third column of that Schedule.

Short title, construction and collective citation

7.—(1) This Act may be cited as the Civil Liability (Amendment) Act 1964.

(2) The Principal Act and this Act shall be construed together as one Act and may be cited together as the Civil Liability Acts 1961 and 1964.

SCHEDULE

ENACTMENTS REPEALED

Number and Year (1)	Short Title (2)	Extent of Repeal (3)
No. 6 of 1957	Statute of Limitations 1957	Paragraph (a) of subsection (4) of section 49.
No. 41 of 1961	Civil Liability Act 1961	Paragraph (c) of subsection (1) of section 40; paragraph (d) of subsection (1) of section 49.

Appendices

APPENDIX ONE

Timothy Dennehy v. Nordic Cold Storage Limited: High Court, Hamilton P. (*ex tempore*), May 8, 1991.

Damages – Personal Injuries – Deductions – Civil Liability (Amendment) Act 1964 (No. 17), s. 2

2.—In assessing damages in an action to recover damages in respect of a wrongful act (including a crime) resulting in personal injury not causing death, account shall not be taken of–
  (a) any sum payable in respect of the injury under any contract of insurance,
  (b) any pension, gratuity or other like benefit payable under statute or otherwise in consequence of the injury.

When an employee while absent from work due to an injury receives a regular payment of monies from his employer pursuant to a non-contributory income protection plan and subsequently sues his employer for, *inter alia*, loss of earnings and the employer is still indemnified pursuant to a contract of insurance for any such payments made pursuant to any such income protection plan, then such a contract of insurance does not fall within the ambit of section 2 of the 1964 Act and consequently, any monies received by the employee pursuant to any such income protection plan ought to be deducted from any assessment of damages in respect of loss of earnings.

Held by Hamilton P. in deducting £16,800 from a sum of £43,000 claimed by the plaintiff as loss of earnings, that:

The plaintiff issued proceedings against his employer seeking damages for personal injuries arising out of an accident occurring in the course of his employment with the defendant. The plaintiff was absent from work as a result of these injuries but throughout his absence he received payment in full from his employer of his net wages pursuant to a non-contributory income protection plan provided by his employer. The defendant employer was indemnified pursuant to a contract of insurance for and against any such payments that might be made pursuant to the income protection plan. The plaintiff was not a party to this contract of insurance nor was he a named beneficiary.

The plaintiff was paid £16,800 during the period in which he was absent from work as a result of the injuries. However, he now sought payment of a sum in respect of loss of earnings for a period which includes the period during which he was paid his full wages pursuant to the income protection plan. The question which faced the Court was whether the defendant should be given credit for any sums paid pursuant to the income protection plan.

These monies were the subject matter of the aforementioned contract of insurance, to which the plaintiff was not a party. The plaintiff relied on section 2 of the 1964 Act and argued that as the monies were paid pursuant to a contract of insurance, they ought not to be taken into account in assessing damages. Hamilton P. held that if the legislature intended that any payment made under a contract of insurance was to be removed from consideration in assessing the loss suffered by the plaintiff, the result would be that the plaintiff would recover more than his actual loss. He could not accept that that was its intention. The intention of the legislature was that when an employer enters into a contract of insurance and the employee benefits from that contract, then that employee must give credit for any sums received while absent from work.

Noel Peart S.C. and Paul Sreenan, instructed by Gerald Goldberg & Co., Cork, for the plaintiff;
Henry Hickey S.C. and Michael Gleeson, instructed by Patrick J. O'Shea & Co., Midleton for the defendant.

Reporter's Note:

Hamilton P. stated during the hearing but not in his judgment that:

> "the question in effect is whether I should decide that the intention of the legislature was such that I should imply the words 'to the plaintiff' after 'any monies payable' . . . pursuant to a contract of insurance in section 2."

Pearse Sreenan B.L.

APPENDIX TWO

District Court Rules 1997

Order 42

THIRD PARTY PROCEDURE

Claim against a person not already a party

1. Where in any civil proceedings a defendant

    (*a*) claims against any person not already a party any contribution or indemnity, or

    (*b*) claims against such person any relief or remedy relating to or connected with the original subject matter of the proceedings and substantially the same as some relief or remedy claimed by the plaintiff, or

    (*c*) requires that any question or issue relating to or connected with the original subject matter of the proceedings should be determined not only as between the plaintiff and the defendant but also as between either or both of them and such person,

such defendant may within ten days of the service upon him or her of the civil summons or notice of application (exclusive of the date of such service) issue and serve upon such person a notice (in this Order called a third party notice (Form 42.1 or 42.2, Schedule C, as the case may be), containing a statement of the nature of the claim against the defendant and the nature and grounds of the defendant's claim against the third party or of the question or issue to be determined.

Copy of summons to be served

2. With the third party notice the defendant shall serve upon such person a copy of the civil summons or notice of application.

Copy to be lodged

3. The defendant shall within the period aforesaid give or send by post to the plaintiff or solicitor for the plaintiff and to the Clerk a copy of the third party notice.

Service

4. The provisions of Order 10 of these Rules relating to the service of documents shall apply to the service of a third party notice.

5. Where a third party notice is served upon the person to whom it is issued such person shall, as from the time of service, be a party (in this Order referred to as a third party) with the same rights as if he or she had been duly sued in the ordinary way by the defendant by whom the notice is issued or by the plaintiff.

Notice of Intention to defend

6. Where a third party disputes the claim by the defendant against him or her or the claim by the plaintiff against the defendant such party shall, within ten days of the service of the third party notice, give or send by post to the defendant or solici-

tor for the defendant and to the Clerk notice of intention to defend (in the Form 42.3, Schedule C), and the provisions of Order 41 (relating to Defence, Lodgment and Counterclaim) of these Rules shall *mutatis mutandis* apply in such case. The Clerk shall notify (Form 42.4, Schedule C) the third party of the place, date and time of sitting of the Court for the hearing of the claim.

7. Proceedings on a third party notice may at any stage be set aside by the Court.

Where no notice of intention to defend given

8. Where a third party fails to give notice of intention to defend he or she shall be bound by any decree (including a decree by consent) or decision in the proceedings so far as it is relevant to any claim, question or issue stated in the third party notice.

Court may grant decree of dismiss

9. Where in any civil proceedings a defendant has served a third party notice, the Court may at or after the trial, or if the proceedings are decided otherwise than by trial, on an application by motion grant such decree or dismiss to or against any party or parties as the nature of the case may require.

Execution not to issue without leave

10. Where in civil proceedings a decree is granted against a defendant and a decree is granted to that defendant against a third party, execution shall not issue against the third party without the leave of the Court until the decree against the defendant has been satisfied.

Claim against person already a party

11. Where in any civil proceedings a defendant claims against any person already a person already a party

    (*a*) any contribution or indemnity, or

    (*b*) any relief or remedy relating to or connected with the original subject matter of the proceedings and substantially the same as some relief or remedy claimed by the plaintiff, or

    (*c*) that any question or issue relating to or connected with the original subject matter of the proceedings should be determined not only as between the plaintiff and the defendant but also as between either or both of them and that person,

the defendant may, within ten days of the service upon him or her of the civil summons or notice of application (exclusive of the date of service) issue and serve upon such person a notice in the prescribed form (Form 42.5, Schedule C) containing a statement of the nature and grounds of the defendant's claim or of the question or issue to be determined. This rule shall not apply to any claim which could be made by counterclaim.

Adjournments

12. The Court may at any time adjourn the proceedings to enable service, lodgment or posting of documents or the giving of notice under this Order to be effected.

SCHEDULE C

Form No. 42.1

Ord. 42, r. 1

THIRD PARTY NOTICE

District Court Area of   District No.

Between

.... of ....
                                                                                    Plaintiff

.... of ....
                                                                                    Defendant

.... of ....
                                                                                    Third Party

TAKE NOTICE that these proceedings have been brought by the Plaintiff against the Defendant.

The Plaintiff claims against the Defendant*   *State briefly
                                                                               nature of claim

as appears on the (civil summons) (notice of application) a copy of which is delivered herewith.

The Defendant claims against you to be indemnified against the Plaintiff's claim and the costs of these proceedings or contribution to the extent of the Plaintiff's claim (or) the following relief or remedy, namely,

on the grounds that†   †state briefly
                                                                               grounds of claim

IF YOU DISPUTE THE CLAIM, then, within ten days of the service upon you of this notice (exclusive of the day of service), detach and complete the two forms of Notice of Intention to Defend at the end of this notice, give or send by post one to the Clerk of the Court at ....
and the other to the Defendant or solicitor for the Defendant.

IF YOU GIVE OR SEND THESE NOTICES, the Clerk will notify you of the place, where and the time and date when you and your witnesses (if any) should attend for the Court hearing of the claim.

‡IF YOU PAY THE CLAIM AND COSTS as stated above to the Defendant or   ‡delete where
solicitor for Defendant before the expiration of ten days from the date of service   applicable

upon you of this Notice, all further proceedings will be stayed, you need not attend court and you will avoid further costs.

‡IF YOU ADMIT THE CLAIM and desire time for payment, you should call to the office of the Defendant's Solicitor within 10 days after the service upon you of this notice and sign a consent.

Dated this   day of   19   .

Signed ....
Defendant or Solicitor
for Defendant

of

To

of

(Third Party)

NOTICES OF INTENTION TO DEFEND as in Form 42.3

SCHEDULE C

Form No. 42.2

Ord. 42, r. 1

THIRD PARTY NOTICE

District Court Area of   District No.

Between

.... of ....
                                                                                    Plaintiff

.... of ....
                                                                                    Defendant

.... of ....
                                                                                    Third Party

    TAKE NOTICE that these proceedings have been brought by the Plaintiff against the Defendant. The Plaintiff claims against the Defendant*   **State briefly nature of claim*

as appears on the (civil summons) (notice of application) copy of which is delivered herewith.

    The Defendant claims that the following question or issue   †*state briefly question or issue to be determined*

should be determined not only as between the Plaintiff and the Defendant but also as between the Plaintiff and the Defendant and you.

    IF YOU DISPUTE THE CLAIM, then, within ten days of the service upon you of this notice (exclusive of the day of service) detach and complete the two forms of Notice of Intention to Defend at the end of this notice, give or send by post one to the Clerk of the Court at ....
and the other to the Defendant or Solicitor for Defendant.

    IF YOU GIVE OR SEND THESE NOTICES, the Clerk will notify you of the place where and the time and date when you and your witnesses (if any) should attend for the Court hearing of the claim.

    ‡IF YOU PAY THE CLAIM AND COSTS as stated above to the Defendant or Solicitor for Defendant before the expiration of ten days from the date of service upon you of this Notice all further proceedings will be stayed and you will avoid further costs.   ‡*delete if applicable*

‡IF YOU ADMIT THE CLAIM and desire time for payment, you should call to the office of the Defendant's Solicitor within 10 days after the service upon you of this notice and sign a consent.

Dated this   day of   19   .

Signed ....
Defendant or Solicitor
for Defendant

of

To

of

(Third Party)

NOTICES OF INTENTION TO DEFEND as in Form 42.3

SCHEDULE C

Form No. 42.3

Ord. 42, r. 6

NOTICE OF INTENTION TO DEFEND

(To be given or sent to the Defendant or Solicitor for Defendant)

District Court Area of   District No.

Between

.... of ....
                                                                                          Plaintiff

.... of ....
                                                                                          Defendant

.... of ....
                                                                                          Third Party

The Third Party intends to defend *(the Defendant's claim against him/her)   *delete where
                                                                                    applicable
*(the Plaintiff's claim against the Defendant)

  Dated this   day of   19   .

                              Signed   ....
                                            Third Party or Solicitor
                                               for Third Party

To the Defendant or Defendant's Solicitor,

of   .

NOTICE OF INTENTION TO DEFEND

(To be given or sent to the District Court Clerk)

District Court Area of   District No.

Between

.... of ....
                                                                                          Plaintiff

.... of ....
                                                                                          Defendant

.... of ....
                                                                                          Third Party

*delete
where
applicable The Third Party intends to defend *(the Defendant's claim against him/her)

*(the Plaintiff's claim against the Defendant)
    Dated this   day of   19   .

                    Signed ....
                              Third Party or Solicitor
                                for Third Party

To the Clerk of the District Court

at

SCHEDULE C

Form No. 42.4

Ord. 42, r. 6

NOTICE OF HEARING

District Court Area of   District No.

Between

.... Plaintiff

.... Defendant

.... Third Party

    TAKE NOTICE that the above proceedings have been listed for hearing at the
sitting of the District Court to be held at ....
on the   day of   19   , at   a.m./p.m.

    Dated this   day of   19   .

                    Signed ....
                              Clerk of the District Court

To

of

Third Party or Solicitor for Third Party

APPENDIX THREE

Rules of the Superior Courts

Order 58, Rule 22

APPEALS TO THE SUPREME COURT

22. Where a defendant desires to contest as respondent, in pursuance of the Civil Liability Act 1962, section 32(3), an appeal brought by a co-defendant, he shall serve notice of his intention to do so in the Form 30 in Appendic C upon such co-defendant and the plaintiff, and upon any other party directly affected thereby, within seven days from the date on which the notice of appeal was served upon him, or within such extended time as may be allowed by the Supreme Court and shall lodge a copy of the notice of intention to contest the appeal wtih the Registrar of the Supreme Court at latest upon the day after the last service of such notice.

APPENDIX C

Form 30

[Title of action]

The notice that the defendant, *E.F.*, intends to contest as respondent, in pursuance of the Civil Liability Act 1961, sectin 32(3), the appeal brought by the defendant, *C.D.*, against the judgment in this action.

        Dated
        (Signed)

To

APPENDIX FOUR

Rules of the Superior Courts

Order 16

THIRD-PARTY PROCEDURE.

1. (1) Where in any action a defendant claims as against any person not already a party to the action (in this Order called "the third-party")—

    (*a*) that he is entitled to contribution or indemnity, or

    (*b*) that he is entitled to any relief or remedy relating to or connected with the original subject matter of the action and substantially the same as some relief or remedy claimed by the plaintiff, or

    (*c*) that any question or issue relating to or connected with the said subject matter is substantially the same as some question or issue arising between the plaintiff and the defendant and should properly be determined not only as between the plaintiff and the defendant but as between the plaintiff and the defendant and the third-party or between any or either of them,

the Court may give leave to the defendant to issue and serve a third-party notice and may, at the same time, if it shall appear desirable to do so, give the third-party liberty to appear at the trial and take such part therein as may be just, and generally give such directions as to the Court shall appear proper for having any question or the rights or liabilities of the parties most conveniently determined and enforced and as to the mode and extent in or to which the third-party shall be bound or made liable by the decision or judgment in the action.

(2) The application for such leave shall be made by motion on notice to the plaintiff. Unless the plaintiff wishes to add the third party as a defendant, his attendance at the hearing of the motion shall not be necessary. If he does attend, he shall not be entitled to costs except by special direction of the Court.

(3) Applicition for leave to issue the third-party notice shall, unless otherwise ordered by the Court, be made within twenty-eight days from the time limited for delivering the defence or, where the application is made by the defendant to a counterclaim, the reply.

2. (1) The third-party notice shall state the nature and grounds of the claim or the nature of the question or issue sought to be determined and the nature and extent of any relief or remedy claimed and any directions of the Court given under rule 1(1) hereof. It shall be in accordance with the Form No. 1 or the Form No. 2 in Appendix C, and shall be sealed, and served on the third-party, and a copy thereof filed with the proper officer in the same manner as in the case of an originating summons.

(2) The notice shall, unless otherwise ordered by the Court, be served within twenty-eight days from the making of the order, and with it there shall he served a copy of the originating summons and of any pleadings delivered in the action.

3. The third-party shall, as from the time of the service upon him of the notice, be a party to the action with the same rights in respect of defence against any claim

made against him and otherwise its if he had been duly sued in the ordinary way by the defendant.

4. (1)   The third-party may enter an appearance in the action within eight days from service or within such further time as may be directed by the Court and specified in the notice: Provided that the third-party failing to appear within such time may apply to the Court for leave to appear, and such leave may be given upon such terms, if any, as the Court may think fit. The memorandum of appearance shall be in the Form No. 3 in Appendix A, Part II.

(2)   Where a third party has entered an appearance and has requested a statement of claim, the defendant shall deliver a statement of claim to the third party within twenty-one days from the entry of appearance.

(3)   Where a third-party has entered an appearance he shall deliver his defence—

    (a)   in case he has not by notice requested a statement of claim, within twenty-eight days from the entry of appearance; or

    (b)   in case he has requested a statement of claim, within twenty-eight days from the date of delivery of the statement of claim.

5.   If a third-party duly served with a third-party notice does not enter an appearance or makes default in delivering any pleading which he has been ordered or is bound to deliver, he shall be deemed to admit the validity of and shall be bound by any judgment given in the action, whether by consent or otherwise, and by any decision therein on any question specified in the notice; and when contribution or indemnity or other relief or remedy is claimed against him in the notice; he shall be deemed to admit his liability in respect of such contribution or indemnity or other relief or remedy.

6.   Where a third-party makes default in entering an appearance or delivering any pleading which he has been ordered or is bound to deliver and the defendant giving the notice suffers judgment by default, such defendant shall be entitled at any time, after satisfaction of the judgment against himself, or before such satisfaction by leave of the Court, to enter judgment against the third-party to the extent of any contribution or indemnity claimed in the third-party notice, or, by leave of the Court, to enter such judgment in respect of any other relief or remedy claimed as the Court shall direct: provided that it shall be lawful for the Court to set aside or vary such judgment against the third-party upon such terms as may seem just.

7.   After the third-party enters an appearance, and before the expiration of the time limited for delivery of defence, he may, after serving notice of the intended application upon the plaintiff and all defendants, apply to the Court to vary any directions given by the Court under sub rule (1) of rule 1 of this Order.

8. (1)   After the third-party has delivered his defence, the defendant giving notice may, after serving notice of the intended application upon the plaintiff, the third-party and any other defendant, apply to the Court for directions and the Court may—

    (a)   where the liability of the third-party to the defendant giving the notice is established on the hearing of the application, order such judgment as the nature of the case may require to be entered against the third-party in favour of the defendant giving the notice, or (*b*) if satisfied that there is a question or issue proper to be tried as between the plaintiff and the defendant and the third-party or between any or either of them as to the liability of the defendant to the plaintiff or as to the liability of the third-party to make any contribution or indemnity claimed in whole or in part, or as to any other relief or remedy claimed in the notice by the defendant, or that a question or issue stated in the notice should be determined not only as between the plaintiff and the defendant but as between the plaintiff, the defendant and the third-party or any or either of them, thereupon try such question or issue or order it to be tried in such manner as the Court may direct, or

(*c*) If it shall appear desirable to do so, give the third-party liberty to defend the action, either alone or jointly with the original defendant, upon such terms as may be just, or

(*d*) dismiss the application.

(2) Any directions given pursuant to this rule may be given either before or after any judgment has been obtained by the plaintiff against the defendant in the action, and may be varied from time to time or rescinded.

(3)   The third-party proceedings may at any time be set aside by the Court.

9. (1) Where the action is tried, the Court which tries the action may, at or after the trial, give such judgment as the nature of the case may require for or against the defendant giving the notice against or for the third-party, and may grant to the defendant or to the third-party any relief or remedy which might properly have been granted if the third-party had been made a defendant to an action duly instituted against him by the defendant: provided that execution shall not be issued against the third-party without leave of the Court until after satisfaction by the defendant of any judgment against him.

(2) Where the action is decided otherwise than by trial, the Court may, on application therefor, make such order as the nature of the case may require, and, where the plaintiff has recovered judgment against the defendant, may order such judgment as may be just to be entered for or against the defendant giving notice against or for the third-party.

10. The Court may decide all questions of costs as between a third-party and the other parties to the action, and may order any one or more to pay the costs of any other or others or give such directions as to costs as the justice of the case may require.

11. (1) Where a third-party makes as against any person not already a party to the action such a claim as is defined in rule 1 the provisions of this Order regulating the rights and procedure as between the defendant and the third-party shall apply *mutatis mutandis* as between the third-party and such other person and the Court may give leave to such third-party to issue a third-party notice, and the preceding rules of this Order shall apply, *mutatis mutandis,* and the expression "third-party notice" and "third-party" shall apply to and include every notice so issued and every person served with such notice respectively.

(2) Where a person served with a notice under this rule by a third-party in turn makes such a claim as is defined in rule 1 against another person not already a party to the action, this Order as applied by this rule shall have effect as regards such further person and any further person or persons so served and so on successively.

12. (1) Where a defendant claims another defendant—

    (*a*) that he is entitled to contribution or indemnity, or

    (*b*) that he is entitled to any relief or remedy relating to or connected with the original subject matter of the action and substantially the same as some relief or remedy claimed by the plaintiff, or

    (*c*) that any question or issue relating to or connected with the said subject matter is substantially the same as some question or issue arising between the plaintiff and the defendant making the claim and should properly be determined not only as between the plaintiff and the defendant making the claim but as between the plaintiff and the defendant and the other defendant or between any or either of them,

the defendant making the claim may, without any leave, issue and serve on such other defendant a notice making such claim or specifying such question or issue. No appearance to such notice shall be necessary.

(2) After service of such notice either defendant shall be at liberty to apply for directions as regards pleadings between them if either considers it necessary to do so. In default of such application within twenty-eight days of service of such notice, the claim, question or issue shall be tried at or after the trial of the plaintiff's action as the trial judge shall direct.

(3) Nothing herein contained shall prejudice the rights of the plaintiff against any defendant to the action.

13. In this Order the words "plaintiff" and "defendant" respectively, shall include a plaintiff and a defendant to a counterclaim.

APPENDIX A, PART II

Form No. 2

Ord. 12, r. 21

MEMORANDUM OF APPEARANCE LIMITING DEFENCE.

(Heading as in Summons).

Enter an appearance for   in this action. The said   limits his defence to part only of the property mentioned in the originating summons, namely, to *the close, called "The Big Field."*

Dated
(Signed)

To

APPENDIX A, PART II

Form No. 3

Ord. 12, r. 21

MEMORANDUM OF APPEARANCE TO THIRD-PARTY NOTICE.

(Heading as in Summons).

Enter an appearance for   to the third party notice issued in this action
on the day of   19 by

       Dated
       (Signed)

APPENDIX C

Form No. 1

Ord. 16, r. 2(1)

THIRD-PARTY NOTICE CLAIMING INDEMNITY OR CONTRIBUTION OR OTHER RELIEF OR REMEDY.
THE HIGH COURT.

               19 No.
Between *A.B.*,   Plaintiff,
and *C.D.*,   Defendant.
and *E.F.*   Third-party.

THIRD-PARTY NOTICE.

Issued pursuant to the order of   dated the   day of 19

To *E. F.* of   in the   of

Take notice that this action has been brought by the plaintiff against the defendant. In it the plaintiff claims against the defendant *[here state concisely the nature of the plaintiff's claim]* as appears by the indorsement on the summons *[or statement of claim]* a copy whereof is delivered herewith.

  The defendant claims against you to be indemnified against the plaintiff's claim and the costs of this action *or* contribution to the extent of *[one half]* of the plaintiff's claim *or* the following relief or remedy namely   on the grounds that *[state concisely the grounds of the claim against the third-party].*

  And take notice that if you wish to dispute the plaintiff's claim against the defendant, or the defendant's claim against you, you are required to enter an appearance within eight days after the service of this notice upon you.

And take notice that the Court has given the following directions under the said order dated the

[and here set out the directions]

If you wish to apply to the Court to vary any of the said directions, you may do so after entering an appearance and before the expiration of the time limited for delivery of your defence under Order 16.

In default of you entering such appearance, you will be deemed to admit the plaintiff's claim against the defendant and the defendant's claim against you and your liability to *[indemnify the defendant or to contribute to the extent claimed or to   stating the relief or remedy sought]* and the validity of any judgment that may be given in the action and you will be bound by such judgment and such judgment may be enforced against you pursuant to Order 16 of the Rules of the Superior Courts.

> Dated
> (Signed)
>> Solicitor for the defendant.

Appearance is to be entered at the Central Office, Four Courts, Dublin.

APPENDIX C

Form No. 2

Ord. 16, r. 2(1)

THIRD-PARTY NOTICE WHEN QUESTION OR ISSUE TO BE DETERMINED

[Title, &c., as in Form No. I down to,* and proceed,]

The defendant claims that the following question or issue, viz.:

[here state concisely the question or issue to be determined] should be determined not only as between the plaintiff and the defendant but as between the plaintiff and the defendant and yourself.

And take notice that if you wish to be heard on the said question or issue or to dispute the defendant's liability to the plaintiff or your liability to the defendant you are required to enter an appearance within eight days after service of this notice.

And take notice that the Court has given the following directions under the said order dated the

[and here set out the direction]

If you wish to apply to the Court to vary any of the said directions you may do so after entering an appearance and before the expiration of the time limited for delivery of your defence under Order 16.

In default of your entering such appearance you will be deemed to admit the validity of and will be bound by any decision or judgment arrived at or given in this action on the said question or issue and to admit any consequent liability of yourself and judgment may be given against you and enforced pursuant to Order 16 of the Rules of the Superior Courts.

Dated
(Signed)

Appearance is to be entered *[&c., as in Form No. 1]*

APPENDIX C

Form No. 1

Ord. 16, r. 2(1)

NOTICE OF COUNTER-CLAIM.

[Title of action].

To the within-named X.Y.

Take notice that if you do not appear to the within counter-claim of the within-named *C.D.* within ten days from the service of this defence and counter-claim upon you, you will be liable to have judgment given against you in your absence.

Appearance is to be entered [*&c., as in Form No. 1*]

Index

Accord and satisfaction
  clarification of law, 19, 20
Air Navigation and Transport Act 1936
  amendment of provisions, 66
Appeal
  concurrent wrongdoers, against, 38

Bankruptcy
  claims, set-off of, 46, 47
  one wrongdoer, of, 53
  proof of claims for damages or contribution in, 74
Breach of statutory duty
  delegation of performance, abolition of defence, 66

Civil liability
  reform of law, 3
Civil Liability Act 1961
  construction, 3
  drafting, 3
  interpretation, 5, 6
  purpose of, 3
  repeals, 6, 77, 78
  savings, 6
Concurrent fault
  contributory negligence. *See* **Contributory negligence**
  defective products, liability for, 11
  fault, meaning, 12, 13
  maritime cases, in, 56, 57
  restitution, provision for, 55, 56
  statutory provisions, 4
  wrongdoers. *See* **Concurrent wrongdoers**
Concurrent wrongdoers
  appeal against, 38
  apportionment of damages, 17, 18
  apportionment of liability, 13–16
  causal responsibility, absence of, 11
  contribution between,
    amount of, 22–24
    appeals, 38
    bankruptcy, proof of claim in, 73
    breach of strict duty, application in case of, 54, 55

Concurrent wrongdoers—*contd.*
  contribution between—*contd.*
    cause of action statute barred, where, 25
    claim in action for, 26–29
    contribution in respect of, 26, 27
    costs, for, 26
    damages, in respect of, 22–24
    damages, regarded as, 38, 39
    discretion to refuse making of order, 31
    enforcement of judgment for, 25
    establishment of right to, 22, 23
    estoppel where claimed, 34–36
    evidence in action, 38
    failure to obtain satisfaction, distribution of loss on, 34
    legal incidents of claim, 37
    limitation of actions, 37
    one-sided periods of limitation, pleading, 55
    one wrongdoer omitted from claim, where, 26, 27
    procedure for claiming, 26–34, 84
    property restored to owner, where, 27
    res judicata rule, 35, 36
    settling tortfeasor, claimed by, 24
    third-party notice, service of, 28–34
  contributory negligence by plaintiff, effect on liability, 50–52
  costs against, 15
  discharge and estoppel by satisfaction, 19
  discontinuance of action, 21, 22
  extent of liability, 13–16
  joinder, 16
  judgment by default against one of, 18
  libel, in relation to, 11
  maritime cases, in, 56, 57
  nuisance, acts constituting, 14

Concurrent wrongdoers—*contd.*
one of,
  bankruptcy of, 53
  judgment against, 20, 21
  judgment in favour of, 21, 22
  limitation of action against, 22
payment into court, taking, 20
persons being, 11–14
release of or accord with one of,
  19, 20
restitution, provision for, 55, 56
separate actions against, 15, 16
several judgments against, 16–18
Consortium, loss of,
contributory negligence, effect of,
  45, 46
Conspiracy
tort, to commit, 12, 13
Contribution
concurrent wrongdoers, between.
  See **Concurrent wrongdoers**
third-party, claim against, 23
Contributory negligence
apportionment of liability in case
  of,
  children, test for, 42
  common law, at, 40
  comparative blameworthiness
    approach, 41, 42
  degree of fault, according to,
    39–44
  entirety, in, 42
  impossibility of establishing
    degrees of fault, 39, 42
  last clear chance, doctrine of,
    40
  person not party to action, to, 41
  voluntary assumption of risk,
    39, 42–44
breach of strict duty, application in
  case of, 54, 55
causation and fault distinguished,
  41
concurrent wrongdoers, liability of,
  50–53
costs in cases of, 54
courts of limited jurisdiction,
  action in, 54
defective products, in relation to,
  44
determining, identification of
  plaintiff, 44–46

Contributory negligence—*contd.*
estoppel in case of, 47–50
last clear chance rule, 66
loss of consortium, damages for,
  45, 46
maritime cases, in, 56, 57
meaning, 39
negligent or careless failure to
  mitigate damage as, 44
one-sided periods of limitation,
  pleading, 55
onus of proof, 41
res judicata, 47–50
restitution, provision for, 55, 56
seat belt, failure to wear, 41
special findings, 53
Costs
contribution in respect of, 25,
  26
contributory negligence, in cases of,
  54
plaintiff an infant, where, 75, 76
third-party, of, 34

Damages
bankruptcy, proof of claim in, 74
charitable payments, deductibility
  of, 82
concurrent wrongdoers,
  contribution between. *See*
  Concurrent wrongdoers
courts of limited jurisdiction, action
  in, 54
exemplary, 7, 8, 18
fatal injuries, for. *See* **Fatal injuries**
insurance moneys, deductibility of,
  80–83
provision of services by defendant
  tortfeasor, effect of, 82, 83
social welfare payments,
  deductibility of, 83
sums not to be taken into account in
  assessing, 80–83
Death
causes of action, survival of,
  common law, at, 3
  damages, scope of, 7–9
  deceased persons,
    subsisting against, 9
    vested in, 7–9
excepted cause of action, meaning,
  7

Death—*contd.*
insolvency of estate against
proceedings maintainable, effect
of, 10, 11
other statutory provisions, under,
9
rights, additional, 8
statutory exceptions, 4
time limit, 9, 10
fatal injuries. *See* **Fatal injuries**
Default judgment
one of concurrent wrongdoers,
against, 18
Defective products
concurrent liability for, 11
contributory negligence in case of,
44

Estoppel
contribution claimed, where, 34–36
contributory negligence, in case of,
47–50

Fatal injuries
damages for,
amount of, 60–64
date of death, running from, 63
division of, 61
divorced spouse, mental distress
of, 64
facts existing at date of death,
ascertained by reference to,
63
funeral and other expenses, for,
61, 64
loss of domestic services, for,
62, 63
mental distress, for, 60–64
pecuniary loss, for, 61, 62
sums not to be taken into
account in assessing, 64, 65
definitions, 57–59
right of action,
cohabitants, of, 58
original, 58
person *in loco parentis*, of, 58,
59
wrongful act, neglect or default,
death caused by, 59, 60
statutory provisions, 4
statutory references, adaptation of,
65

Indemnity
third-party, claim against, 23
Infant
plaintiff being, costs in actions,
75–76
Insolvency
estate against which action
maintainable, of, 10, 11
Insurance
moneys payable under policies of,
application of, 74, 75
set-off deduction, recovery of, 46,
47

Libel
concurrent wrongdoers, 11
damages, mitigation of, 17
Limitation of actions
concealed fraud, on, 22
conspiracy to commit tort, in
respect of, 12, 13
contribution, for, 36, 37
estate of deceased person, action
against, 9, 10
one concurrent wrongdoer, against,
22
one-sided periods of, pleading,
55
Local authority
non-feasance, liability for, 73

Mechanically propelled vehicle
belonging to State, wrong
committed by, 70, 71
damages for personal injuries
relating to use of, 83

Negligence
last opportunity rule, 66
Nuisance
acts of two or more persons
causing, 14

Payment into court
infant plaintiff, acceptance by,
75–76
Payment out of court
one concurrent wrongdoer, paid in
by, 20
Personal representative
same right of action as deceased,
having, 4

Road authority
  meaning, 72
  public road, liability for failure to
    maintain, 71–73

Set-off
  claims, of, 46, 47, 83
Settlement
  contribution, claim of, 24

Third-party notice
  contribution, claim for, 27–32
  costs, questions of, 34
  delay, effect of, 32
  discretion of court to issue, 32,
    33
  estoppel where contribution
    claimed, 34, 35
  leave to serve, 34
  third-party not within jurisdiction,
    where, 33

Tort
  defence that plaintiff in breach of
    civil or criminal law, abolition,
    67–70
  illegality, doctrine of, 67–70
  unborn child, wrongs to, 70
Tortfeasors
  concurrent fault. *See* **Concurrent
    fault; Concurrent wrongdoers**
  joint and several, abolition of
    distinction, 12

Unborn child
  wrongs to, 70

Vessel
  damage to, concurrent fault for, 56,
    57

Workmen's compensation
  amendment of provisions, 66